Published in 2007 by Stewart, Tabori & Chang
An imprint of Harry N. Abrams, Inc.

Library of Congress Cataloging-in-Publication Data:
Barr, Lynne.
  Knitting new scarves / by Lynne Barr.
      p. cm.
  ISBN-13: 978-1-58479-633-6
  ISBN-10: 1-58479-633-2
  1. Knitting--Patterns. 2. Scarves. I. Title.

TT825.B2975 2007
746.43'2041--dc22

2006101806

Editor: Melanie Falick
Designer: Sarah Von Dreele
Production Manager: Jacqueline Poirier

The text of this book was composed in Futura
and Mrs Eaves.

Printed and bound in China

10 9 8 7 6 5 4 3 2 1

HNA
harry n. abrams, inc.
a subsidiary of La Martinière Groupe

115 West 18th Street
New York, NY 10011
www.hnabooks.com

KNITTING NEW SCARVES

27 DISTINCTLY MODERN DESIGNS

LYNNE BARR

PHOTOGRAPHS BY TYLLIE BARBOSA

PHOTO-STYLING BY KELLY McKAIG

TABLE OF CONTENTS

INTRODUCTION

It has been a long time since I've taught a knitting workshop, but while writing this book, I've thought often of students from a beginning knitting class. I don't think my class was what they expected and I was certainly surprised by them as well. At our first meeting I announced that they were going to design their own projects. They learned to cast on, knit, and purl. They learned to recognize knit and purl stitches, and how to distinguish between them, whether looking at an actual piece of knitting, or at pictures of stitch patterns in a book.

The process of becoming "knit literate" had begun. As soon as they learned these basics, I encouraged them to become creative knitters. They would return to class with smiles from ear to ear and samples of their discoveries. At one of the early classes, one student surprised me when he unrolled about three feet of stitch samples, comprised entirely of different combinations of knit and purl stitches. Some were the common checkerboard-like moss stitch and rib varieties, but a few patterns may have been uniquely his. Whatever knitting mishaps occurred for these new knitters—dropped or twisted stitches, unintentional decreases or increases—we looked at them and figured out what had happened. They weren't mistakes; they were opportunities.

My hope for this book is that it inspires other knitters to pick up yarn and needles and just play, finding ways to make new forms and discover new connections. When you look at one of my scarves, ask yourself, "What if?" It's a question I constantly ask myself when playing with an idea. You might notice similarities between some of the scarf directions, and then how a single change created a whole new look. For instance, when I completed Meandering Stripes (page 62), I asked myself "What if I added short rows to create sharper curves, or eliminated all curves to the right to create a scarf that would only spiral leftward in a coil." Neither of those ideas developed into a pattern, but changing the number of colors and increasing the size of each wedge resulted in

Stacked Wedges (page 90). The new scarf has a subtler curve, and instead of a striped appearance, it has become a multicolored patchwork. While knitting your new scarves, I invite you to try other possibilities and to ask some of the other questions I ask myself: "What if I switch these stitches, or turn in this direction instead of that, or divide some of these stitches instead of all of them, or move stitches forward instead of backward?" The possibilities are endless!

Knitting is certainly as much about a process as a finished product. Otherwise, we would all purchase finished knit items that probably cost less these days than purchasing yarn. I do take pride in the scarves I designed and knit for this book, but it doesn't come close to the excitement I felt when I would wake at five in the morning with an idea I wanted to try. After a quick pass through the kitchen to make a cup of coffee, I was eager to pick up needles and yarn to work out my vision. It is my hope that knitters who use this book will be inspired to take chances, and will use these patterns as a leaping off point for their own exciting creations.

While friends were testing my patterns, they would often ask, "How did you think of this one?" More often than not, my answer was the name of a building. I was probably influenced more by architecture than anything else. When excited by a building, I want to travel there to see it and experience the space. Some of the scarves in this book are the result of me working out those desires in yarn—see Twisted (page 114) and Tricorner (page 108), which came from my appreciation of the Infinity Tower in

Dubai, United Arab Emirates, and Circles (page 22), which was inspired by a freeform house in California. The knitting in the photo above was inspired by a building in Milan that has an organically-shaped glass ceiling, the center of which curves to the floor, creating a funnel shape in the interior space. The sky and clouds above it appear to be pulled into the funnel, connecting them to the interior floor.

Translating geometric shapes from architecture, normally used for their structural rigidity, into the soft medium of yarn provided me a mild challenge. My greater challenge was to convert these now pliable forms into scarves that would wrap around a neck without looking preposterous! The greatest challenge of all was forcing myself to put down my yarn and needles in order to write the patterns. I hope you enjoy them, but mostly I hope they help you to kindle new ideas of your own.

Before You Start

A Note on Techniques

Near the start of each pattern you will see a list of the techniques required. All of these techniques—there are ten of them—are explained in detail at the back of the book (beginning on page 126). Some of them, like Intarsia and Short Row Shaping, are very common; others, like Rib Division (a way of dividing up knit and purl stitches so they can be worked separately for a while and then can be reconnected later) and Interlocking Stitches (a method for attaching stitches from a finished piece to stitches live on a needle) may be new to many knitters. All of these techniques are used in scarves throughout the book. In addition, within some of the patterns, you will find further instruction for techniques that are only used for that specific scarf (though, of course, you can choose to apply them in your own designs as you like).

To avoid having to flip back and forth between the actual scarf patterns and the technique instructions given at the back of the book, I suggest that you photocopy the technique pages you need from the back and then place them next to the pattern instructions you are following. Before too long the new techniques will become second nature and you will not need the photocopies, but until that happens, I think you will find this setup helpful.

A Few Words About Ribs

Since my primary interest was in form and structure, I didn't spend time creating decorative stitch patterns for the scarves. Most of them are simply worked in Garter for its ability to hold a shape, and Rib for its efficacy in shaping by dividing and combining stitches. I don't have anything to add about Garter, but I do have a few words about Ribs.

I've considered why, in spite of efforts to avoid it, ribs spread and practically double in width for some knitters but not others. My current theory is that it's due to how the working yarn is carried back and forth between the needles when changing from purl to knit. A stable rib does not depend on tightly wrapping the yarn around a needle when making a new stitch. Trying to work tight stitches will just make it hard to maintain a consistent stitch gauge. But, you do need to add some tension when carrying yarn between needles to avoid slack between stitches. It's the slack yarn between stitches that causes the spread. This explanation works for me, but I'm sure there are other knitters with other theories to share.

Skill Levels

I haven't assigned a skill level to the individual patterns, because I think this is best judged by each of you. I have tried to include what I think is a range of patterns from easy to challenging. Reading through the introductions I've written for each scarf may help you decide which scarf is right for your abilities, and only you know how much of a challenge you're in the mood for. This book is about knitting "new" scarves—that is, thinking about what scarves are and how they can be knit in new ways. So when you come upon a concept or technique that is new to you, I hope you will embrace it. Though some of these scarves take more concentration than others, I assure you that all of them are exciting to create once you get going.

Aria

This scarf was inspired by a spectacular, broad-leafed seaweed with fluttering edges called Laminaria. I wanted it to be more than just a large ruffle, so I created a wide central core with narrow rippled edges. If you prefer a narrower scarf, you can easily decrease the width by eliminating some of the central Garter stitches.

FINISHED MEASUREMENTS

7" wide x 46" long (or 52" if worked using 3 hanks B)

YARN

Karabella Yarns Aurora 8 (100% merino wool; 98 yards / 50 grams): 4 balls #5 Red (A)

Koigu Painter's Palette Premium Merino (KPPPM) (100% merino wool; 175 yards / 50 grams): 2 hanks #P816 (B) (or 3 hanks if you work 52" length)

NEEDLES

One pair 10" straight needles size US 9 (5.5 mm)

Change needle size if necessary to obtain correct gauge.

GAUGE

13½ sts = 4" (10 cm) in Garter stitch (knit every row), with 1 strand each of A and B held together

TECHNIQUE

Short Row Shaping (see page 140)

With one strand each of A and B held together, CO 30 sts.

Work Pattern followed by Reverse Pattern.

PATTERN

ROW 1: P6, K1-tbl, K16, K1-tbl, K6.
ROW 2: Repeat Row 1.
ROW 3: P5, W&T, K5 back to side edge.
ROW 4: P3, W&T, K3 back to side edge.
ROW 5: P6, hiding wraps, K1-tbl, K16, K1-tbl, K6.
ROWS 6-8: Repeat Rows 3-5.
ROW 9: P6, K1-tbl, K16, K1-tbl, K6.
ROW 10: Repeat Row 9.

REVERSE PATTERN

ROW 1: K6, K1-tbl, K16, K1-tbl, P6.
ROW 2: Repeat Row 1.
ROW 3: K5, W&T, P5 back to side edge.
ROW 4: K3, W&T, P3 back to side edge.
ROW 5: K6, hiding wraps, K1-tbl, K16, K1-tbl, P6.
ROWS 6-8: Repeat Rows 3-5.
ROW 9: K6, K1-tbl, K16, K1-tbl, P6.
ROW 10: Repeat Row 9.

Continue working, alternating Pattern with Reverse Pattern, until the Scarf measures 46" (or 52" if using 3 hanks of B).

BO all sts in the pattern of the last completed row.

BLACK PEARLS

Maybe you would prefer to knit white pearls or multicolored beads. Whichever you choose, you should be aware that people like to squeeze and play with this scarf. Knitting Pearls in public could be hazardous to the progress of your knitting! There is a lot of decreasing and increasing as you knit around, but the knitting progresses rapidly and each completed Pearl brings with it a wonderful sense of accomplishment.

Finished Measurements

Approximately 62" long
Small (Medium, Large) Pearls:
approximately 2" (2½", 3") diameter, stuffed

Yarn and Stuffing

Peace Fleece Worsted Weight Knitting Yarn (70%
wool / 30% mohair; 200 yards / 4 ounces): 2 skeins
Fathers Gray
Peace Fleece Batting (wool / mohair): approximately
8 ounces Fathers Gray, for stuffing

Needles

One set of four 5-6" double-pointed needles (DPN)
size US 8 (5 mm)
Change needle size if necessary to obtain correct gauge.

Notions

Stitch marker

Gauge

17 sts = 4" (10 cm) in Garter stitch (knit 1 rnd,
purl 1 rnd)

Technique

Knitting Around (see page 136)

Notes

Stuff Pearls enough to hold a round shape,
but not so densely that they feel hard.

CO 6 sts; divide sts evenly among 3 needles
[2 sts per needle]. Join for working around,
being careful not to twist sts; place marker for
beg of rnd. Work 8 small, 9 medium, and 8 large
Pearls in order to create scarf shown. Or,
knit Pearls in whatever size and order you like.

Small Pearl

Begin with 6 sts [2 sts on 3 needles].
RND 1: *K1-f/b; rep from * to end of rnd [12 sts].
RNDS 2, 4, 6, 8, 10, 12, 14, AND 16: Purl.
RND 3: *K1, K1-f/b; repeat from * to end of
rnd [18 sts].
RND 5: *K2, K1-f/b; repeat from * to end of
rnd [24 sts].
RNDS 7, 9, 11, AND 13: Knit.
RND 15: *K2, K2tog; repeat from * to end of
rnd [18 sts remain].
RND 17: *K1, K2tog; repeat from * to end of
rnd [12 sts remain]. Stuff Pearl with batting.

RND 18: *P2tog; repeat from * to end of
rnd [6 sts remain]. *Do not break yarn.
Carry yarn from one Pearl to the next.*

Medium Pearl

Begin with 6 sts [2 sts on 3 needles].
RND 1: *K1-f/b; rep from * to end of rnd [12 sts].
RNDS 2, 4, 6, 8, 10, 12, 14, 16, 18, AND 20: Purl.
RND 3: *K1, K1-f/b; repeat from * to end of
rnd [18 sts].
RND 5: *K2, K1-f/b; repeat from * to end of
rnd [24 sts].
RND 7: *K3, K1-f/b; repeat from * to end of
rnd [30 sts].
RNDS 9, 11, 13, AND 15: Knit.
RND 17: *K3, K2tog; repeat from * to end of
rnd [24 sts remain].
RND 19: *K2, K2tog; repeat from * to end of
rnd [18 sts remain].
RND 21: *K1, K2tog; repeat from * to end of
rnd [12 sts remain]. Stuff Pearl with batting.
RND 22: *P2tog; repeat from * to end of rnd
[6 sts remain]. *Do not break yarn.
Carry yarn from one Pearl to the next.*

Large Pearl

Begin with 6 sts [2 sts on 3 needles].
RND 1: *K1-f/b; repeat from * to end of rnd [12 sts].
RNDS 2, 4, 6, 8, 10, 12, 14, 16, 18, 20, AND 22: Purl.
RND 3: *K1, K1-f/b; repeat from * to end of rnd [18 sts].
RND 5: *K1, K1-f/b; repeat from * to end of rnd [27 sts].
RND 7: *K2, K1-f/b; repeat from * to end of rnd [36 sts].
RNDS 9, 11, 13, 15, AND 17: Knit.
RND 19: *K2, K2tog; repeat from * to end of rnd
[27 sts remain].
RND 21: *K1, K2tog; repeat from * to end
of rnd [18 sts remain].
RND 23: *K1, K2tog; repeat from * to end
of rnd [12 sts remain]. Stuff Pearl with batting.
RND 24: *P2tog; repeat from * to end of rnd
[6 sts remain]. *Do not break yarn. Carry yarn from one Pearl
to the next.*

Finishing

Cut yarn after final Pearl, leaving a 6" tail; thread
through remaining sts, pull tight, and fasten off.
Weave in tail at both ends.

Carumboa

Making this scarf is a great way to use up bits of yarn leftover from finished projects. It is also a perfect project for teaching children to knit. If you choose to work with a child on this scarf, I recommend letting the child knit the background sections while you knit the cross-through pieces and interlock them. Eight stitches by seventeen rows should work up in no time for a child, who will quickly move on to a new piece with a different color or yarn, avoiding potential boredom. Cast-on and bind-off instructions will stick with them, because they will have reason to practice those frequently on each new piece. If interest begins to wane before the scarf is long enough to wear, then look for some ribbon to attach to each end and transform it into a necklace.

⊠⧖⊠⧖⊠⧖⊠⧖⊠⧖⊠⧖⊠⧖

FINISHED MEASUREMENTS
Approximately 3" wide x 66" long
Unit length: 1½", when strung on elastic cord
*Note: 8 units will make approximately 12" of Scarf.
Scarf shown is made with 44 units.*

YARN
Harrisville Designs New England Highland
(100% pure wool; 200 yards / 100 grams):
1 hank each #65 Poppy, #66 Melon,
#40 Topaz, #39 Russet, #2 Red,
#46 Oatmeal, #47 Suede, #48 Dove Grey,
#45 Pearl, #50 Black
*Note: This Scarf only used a small portion of
each hank (approximately 15 grams /½ ounce).*

NEEDLES
One pair double-pointed needles (DPN) size
US 8 (5 mm)
Change needle size if necessary to obtain
correct gauge.

GAUGE
16 sts = 4" (10 cm) in Garter stitch
(knit every row)

NOTIONS
Tapestry needle; 1 spool .8 mm clear elastic
cord (available at bead stores and craft stores
that carry beading supplies)

TECHNIQUE
Interlocking Stitches (see page 130)

NOTES
Carumboa is made of 44 individual units
(each consisting of a Background Piece and
Cross-Through Piece) strung together like
beads onto a clear elastic cord.

Make Units
Make an assortment of solid-color and two-color
units. For a solid-color unit, work the Background
and Cross-Through Pieces in the same color.
For a two-color unit, work the Background and
Cross-Through Pieces in different colors. You can
weave in tails on the individual units and string
them onto the cord as you finish them.

BACKGROUND PIECE
CO 8 sts. Work Garter st (knit every row) for 17 rows.
Bind off all sts.

CROSS-THROUGH PIECE
CO 8 sts. Work Garter st for 9 rows. Do not BO sts.

INTERLOCK PIECES
Hold needle with Cross-Through Piece in front of
and halfway up Background Piece. Using Interlocking
Stitches method (see page 130), interlock the two
pieces to make one unit.

Continuing on the sts from Cross-Through Piece,
work in Garter st for 8 rows. BO all sts.

WEAVE UNIT TAILS
Weave in ends through side sts to where pieces
interlock (see Photo 1). Tie tails together and clip
close to knot (see Photo 2).

Assemble Units
Using tapestry needle threaded with clear elastic
cord, thread needle through center of unit, where
pieces interlock, running thread alternately through
one st from Background Piece and one st from
Cross-Through Piece (see Photo 3).

When all units are threaded onto cord, weave ends
of cord back through several end units. Secure
with knot and cut cord close to knot. *Note: If elastic
cord is too stretchy, you may want to weave it back
through all units.*

WEAVING UNIT TAILS AND
ASSEMBLING UNITS

1.

2.

3.

CIRCLES

Here's an eye-catching scarf that usually elicits a range of interpretations, from a comparison to octopus tentacles to a seemingly unrelated craving for little powdered-sugar donuts. Neither tentacles nor donuts were my inspiration, which actually came from the round windows of an exotic freeform house in California. If you love knitting around, you'll be in knitting heaven. Circles requires knitting around for the tubular body of the scarf, and then knitting around again and again for each of the decorative circles.

FINISHED MEASUREMENTS
3¾" wide x 58" long

YARN
Queensland Collection Kathmandu Aran (85% merino wool / 10% silk / 5% cashmere; 104 yards / 50 grams): 2 balls #120 (MC), 1 ball #135 (A)
15 yards lighter weight contrasting color scrap yarn (to be removed and discarded when you make the circle)

NEEDLES
One set of four double-pointed needles (DPN) size US 10 (6 mm)
One set of four double-pointed needles size US 10½ (6.5 mm)
One pair double-pointed needles size US 9 (5.5 mm) or smaller, for opening Scrap Yarn Slits
Change needle size if necessary to obtain correct gauge.

NOTIONS
Stitch marker; tapestry needle

GAUGE
15 sts = 4" (10 cm) in Stockinette stitch (St st) using size US 10 needles

TECHNIQUES
Knitting Around (see page 136)
Scrap Yarn Slits (see page 138)

Using MC and US 10 needles, CO 27 sts; divide sts evenly among 3 needles [9 sts per needle]. Join for working around, being careful not to twist sts; place marker for beg of rnd. Begin St st (knit every rnd). Work even until piece measures 2" from the beginning.

BEGIN PATTERN
RND 1: Needle 1 - K2, set up Scrap Yarn Slit (SYS) across 5 sts (see page 138), K2; Needles 2 and 3 - Knit all sts.
RNDS 2-6, 8-12 AND 14-18: Knit sts on all needles.
RND 7: Needle 1 - Knit all sts; Needle 2 - K2, set up SYS across 5 sts, K2; Needle 3 - Knit all sts.
RND 13: Needles 1 and 2 - Knit all sts; Needle 3 - K2, set up SYS across 5 sts, K2.
Repeat Rnds 1-18 thirteen times.
Knit around for 2", then BO.

MAKE CIRCLES
Work one circle at a time. Using smaller needles, open Scrap Yarn Slits (see page 139) [10 sts].

With a US 10½ needle and A, knit the 5 sts on the lower needle. Insert an empty US 10½ needle from right to left into the edge stitch between the upper and lower needles (see Photo 1).

Twist the needle clockwise and knit the stitch [11 sts] (see Photo 2).

Turn work upside down and knit next 5 sts with an empty US 10½ needle.

Pick up, twist, and knit another edge stitch between the needles [12 sts].

Divide the 12 sts evenly onto 3 US 10½ needles and knit around for 4 rows (see Photo 3).

BO all sts. Cut yarn, leaving 4" tail. Thread tail onto tapestry needle and run through MC st next to circle, to WS of Scarf. Tie both tails of circle together and trim ends. Repeat for remaining circles.

MAKING CIRLCES

Cocoons

This scarf is a series of loosely knit pockets filled
with batting, each separated from the next by
a tightly knit rib. When knit to the length shown
here, Cocoons is more of a decorative accessory
than a functional warm scarf, but it can easily
be lengthened to wrap multiple times around the
neck for greater cold-weather efficacy.

Finished Measurements
4" wide x 48" long

Yarn and Stuffing
Habu Textiles Cotton Linen Cord (54% cotton /
46% linen; 65 yards / 1 ounce): 4 ounces
#11 gray
Habu Textiles Bamboo Fiber (100% bamboo):
2 ounces, for stuffing

Needles
One set of three double-pointed needles (DPN)
size US 8 (5 mm)
One set of three double-pointed needles size
US 10 (6 mm)
One pair double-pointed or single-pointed
needles size US 4 (3.5 mm)
Change needle size if necessary to obtain
correct gauge.

Gauge
15 sts = 4" (10 cm) in Stockinette stitch (St st)
using largest needles

Techniques
Combine Stitches (see page 129)
Rib Division (see page 130)
Knitting Around on Two Double-Pointed Needles
 (see page 137)

Using US 8 DPNs, CO 24 sts. Work in K1, P1 rib,
slipping first K st of each row knitwise.
Work rib for 4 rows.

Make Cocoon Pouch
Using Rib Division method (see page 130),
divide sts onto two DPNs (12 sts each needle).

With US 10 DPNs, knit 12 sts on front needle,
turn and knit 12 sts on next needle (see Knitting
Around on Two Double-Pointed Needles, page 137).
Continue knitting for 3 rounds.

Moderately stuff the Pouch with bamboo fiber
shaped into a cocoon.

Close Cocoon Pouch
With the two needles held parallel in your left
hand, combine stitches from both needles into
a K1, P1 rib (see Combine Stitches, page 129),
using a US 8 DPN. Rib in K1, P1 with US 8 DPNs
for 3 rows, slipping first st of each row knitwise.

Continue working the Scarf, alternating
directions for Make Cocoon Pouch, followed
by Close Cocoon Pouch.

End repeats when Scarf measures approximately
47", by working Close Cocoon Pouch with
US 4 needles instead of US 8 needles. BO all sts.
(The smaller needles are used for BO to keep
end of scarf from flaring.)

Drifting Pleats

When knit with a deliciously soft yarn with beautiful drape such as the wool-silk blend shown here, this pleated scarf is a perfect marriage of material and method. It's probably the most challenging pattern in the book because the directions do not specify stitch numbers; instead, you need to recognize the logic of the stitch sequencing that makes the pleats "drift," as well as manipulate as many as six needles in an unconventional setup. After you work the pleat setup and knit a few rows it gets easier, but it still requires your undivided attention.

Finished Measurements
4" wide x 58" long

Yarn
Alchemy Yarns Sanctuary (70% wool /
30% silk; 125 yards / 50 grams): 3 hanks
#042M Silver

Needles
One set of five 6" double-pointed needles
(DPN) size US 8 (5 mm)
One pair single-pointed needles (SPN)
size US 8 (5 mm)
One double- or single-pointed needle size
US 5 (3.75 mm) (or smaller), for BO
row only
Change needle size if necessary to obtain
correct gauge.

Notions
J-Shaped Cable Needle (J-Needle)

Gauge
18 sts = 4" (10 cm) in Stockinette stitch
(St st) using larger needles

Techniques
Combine Stitches (see page 129)
Rib Division (used only on BO row)
(see page 130)

Notes
Detailed instructions for Setup Pleats, WS
Pleat Row, RS Pleat Row, RS Shift Pleat Row,
and WS Merge Pleat Row are grouped
together at the end of the general pattern
directions.
Except for the WS row in Setup Pleats, the
pattern will always be K1, P1. In other
words, a K will never be next to a K, or a P
next to a P.
It is very important to work with specific
needle (DPN or SPN) indicated in pattern.
This ensures you will be able to work
pattern correctly.
Slip the first stitch of each row knitwise.
This stitch is included in the pattern; it is not
an extra stitch.

With SPN, CO 38 sts.

Scarf Pattern
Work Setup Pleats.

Pleat Pattern
ROW 1: Work a WS Pleat Row.
ROW 2: Work a RS Pleat Row.
ROW 3: Work a WS Pleat Row.
ROW 4: Work a RS Shift Pleat Row.

Repeat Pleat Pattern until you are working Row 4
and 2 sts are on first DPN at right edge. Slip the 2 sts
onto the J-Needle. *(J-Needle is simply a DPN substitute
because 2 sts tend to slip off the DPN.)* After the 2 sts
are transferred to the J-Needle, finish the rest of Row
4 as usual.

For the next repeat of Pleat Pattern, when there are
2 sts on the J-Needle, substitute WS Merge Pleat Row
on Row 3. On Row 4 of this repeat, shift remaining
pleats as usual. If all pleats have been merged, then
eliminate Row 4 of the repeat.

When all pleats have been merged, K1, P1 on all
38 sts for 5 rows, slipping first st of each row knitwise.

Repeat Scarf Pattern 5 times. On last repeat,
discontinue RS Shift Pleat Row when last pleat is
4 sts from edge.

Work Rows 1–3 once more.

On next row (RS), BO 3 sts in rib. Divide sts of pleat
(see Rib Division, page 130). BO remaining st on
right-hand needle and sts on front DPN, then back
DPN (from Rib Division of pleat) knitwise, until
1 st remains on right-hand needle. BO remaining sts
on DPN or SPN in K1, P1 rib with a very small
needle to keep bottom edge of Scarf from ruffling.

Setup Pleats

ROW 1 (WS): With SPN, slip 1 st knitwise, P1, K1, P7, [K1, P1] twice, P6, [K1, P1] twice, P6, [K1, P1] 4 times.

ROW 2: With empty DPN, slip 1 st knitwise, P1, [K1, P1] 3 times. Slip next 3 sts purlwise onto an empty DPN. Slip next 3 sts purlwise onto another empty DPN.

Fold the second DPN with 3 sts clockwise so it is behind and parallel to the first DPN with 3 sts (see Photo 1).

With working DPN, [K1 from front DPN and P1 from back DPN] 3 times to combine the 6 sts (see Combine Stitches, page 129).

With an empty DPN, rib the same 6 sts again, slipping first st knitwise (see Photo 2).

With working DPN, [K1, P1] twice from the SPN. Slip next 3 sts purlwise onto an empty DPN. Slip next 3 sts purlwise onto another DPN. Fold the two DPNs with 3 sts (see Photo 1) and with the working needle combine the 6 sts into another pleat. With an empty DPN, rib the 6 sts of the pleat again, slipping first st knitwise. Repeat from * to * once. With working DPN, [K1, P1] twice across remaining sts on SPN (see Photo 3).

1.

2.

3.

4.

5.

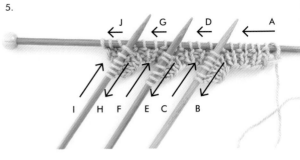

WS Pleat Row

Note: Remember to slip first stitch of row knitwise.

You will be working background sts off each pleat DPN onto an empty SPN. The 6 sts of each pleat are not worked on this row, and will remain on the DPNs.

With empty SPN, *K1, P1 from DPN until 6 sts (one pleat) remain on the DPN. * Repeat from * to * for each DPN except the last. Rib all sts remaining on last DPN. The last DPN does not hold a pleat; all sts on this DPN are background sts.

On a completed WS row, all pleats are on DPNs and all background sts are on the SPN (see Photo 4). As pleats shift and eventually merge into the background, the number of DPNs with pleats will decrease.

RS Pleat Row

Note: Remember to slip first stitch of row knitwise.

Pleats (on DPNs) are worked on both sides, increasing each pleat by 2 rows every RS. Background stitches worked from the SPN are only increased by one row every RS.

The following lettered instructions correspond to Photo 5:

A. With empty DPN, slip 1 st knitwise, P1, [K1, P1] from SPN to pleat.
B. With working DPN, [K1, P1] on 6 sts of pleat.
C. With empty DPN, slip 1 st knitwise, P1, [K1, P1] on sts of same pleat [6 sts].
D. With working DPN, [K1, P1] on next 4 sts of SPN.
E. With working DPN, [K1, P1] on 6 sts of next pleat.
F. With empty DPN, slip 1 st knitwise, P1, [K1, P1] on sts of same pleat [6 sts].
G. With working DPN, [K1, P1] on next 4 sts of SPN.
H. With working DPN, [K1, P1] on 6 sts of next pleat.
I. With empty DPN, slip 1 st knitwise, P1, [K1, P1] on sts of same pleat [6 sts].
J. With working DPN, [K1, P1] for remaining sts of SPN.

Steps A–J are worked when there are 3 pleats. When working a RS Pleat Row after pleat(s) have been merged, not all these steps will be worked.
When 2 pleats remain, work Steps A–F and J for a RS Pleat Row.
When 1 pleat remains, work Steps A–C and J for a RS Pleat Row.

6.

7.

8.

RS Shift Pleat Row
Note: Remember to slip first stitch of row knitwise.

The directional arrows in Photo 5 apply to this row, but each pleat will be shifted two stitches to the right when worked.

With DPN, slip 1 st knitwise, P1, [K1, P1] to 2 sts before pleat. *With working DPN, [K1, P1] on 6 sts of pleat. With empty DPN, slip 1 st knitwise, P1, [K1, P1] on sts of same pleat. With working needle, [K1, P1] twice from SPN (you will be 2 sts before the next pleat). Repeat from * until last pleat is worked. With working needle, rib remaining sts from SPN.

WS Merge Pleat Row
Note: Remember to slip first stitch of row knitwise.

With SPN, work WS Pleat Row up to J-Needle (see Photo 6). Rib the 2 sts on the J-Needle (see Photo 7). Do not turn work. Rib the 6 sts from the inner to the outer edge of the pleat (see Photo 8). These 6 sts are now background sts.

EASY WAVE

I always like to approach my design challenges from different angles. So, after working New Wave (page 66), I was interested in creating another variation of a wavy scarf. I think this one—worked flat on slipped stitches, rather than around using short rows—is a little easier to execute than New Wave, thus its name.

FINISHED MEASUREMENTS
4½" wide x 65" long

YARN
Peace Fleece Worsted Weight Knitting Yarn
(70% wool / 30% mohair; 200 yards / 4
ounces): 2 hanks Fathers Gray

NEEDLES
One set of three double-pointed needles (DPN)
size US 10¾ (7 mm)
Change needle size if necessary to obtain
correct gauge.

GAUGE
14 sts = 4" (10 cm) in Stockinette stitch (St st)

TECHNIQUES
Combine Stitches (see page 129)
Rib Division (see page 130)

CO 24 sts and work K1, P1 rib for 3 rows, slipping first K st of each row knitwise.

*Divide sts onto two needles, slipping last purl st onto front needle with knit sts [13 sts on front needle; 11 sts on back needle] (see Rib Division, page 130). *Note: If you forget to include this last purl st with the knit sts, the scarf edge will not look right.*

Work the 13 sts on the front needle in St st for 4 rows, slipping first st on each row knitwise.

K1 from front needle and P1 from back needle, ending with P1 from front needle, until all 24 sts are worked in a K1, P1 rib onto one needle (see Combine Stitches, page 129).

Rib in K1, P1 for 2 rows, slipping first st of each row knitwise.*

Repeat from * to * until Scarf measures approximately 65".

BO all sts in K1, P1 rib.

FLAPPER

The flaps in this scarf remind me of Venetian
blinds that open and close to reveal or hide
what lies behind them. As the scarf moves and
wraps around the neck, its flaps reveal and hide
the background yarn. There are two tails from
each of the flaps to weave in, and some knitters
may balk at that. But I think tail-weaving is
the perfect task for times when I want to use my
hands without testing my mind.

Finished Measurements
4½" wide x 44" long

Yarn
Peace Fleece Worsted Weight Knitting Yarn
(70% wool / 30% mohair; 200 yards /
4 ounces): 1 skein each Baku Black (MC)
and Fathers Gray (A)

Needles
One set of three double-pointed or short
single-pointed needles size US 10½ (6.5 mm)
Change needle size if necessary to obtain
correct gauge.

Notions
Tapestry needle

Gauge
13 sts = 4" (10 cm) in Garter stitch
(knit every row)

Note
The entire Scarf (Flaps and background) is
worked in Garter stitch.

Leave MC attached throughout entire scarf.
Only A is cut after each Flap is attached.

With MC (background color), CO 15 sts and knit
3 rows. Leave on needle with yarn attached.

Make a Flap
With an empty needle and A (Flap color), CO 15 sts.
Knit 8 rows. Do not BO.

Attach the Flap
With your left hand, hold the needle with Flap
sts (A) in front of the needle with Background
sts (MC). The RS of both pieces should be facing
you (see Photo 1).

With A, knit the sts from both needles together, as
follows: Knit into the first st of the front and back
needles at the same time (see Photo 2); repeat this
process until all sts from both needles have been
worked together.

Knit one more row with A. Cut A, leaving a 3–4" tail.
Do NOT cut MC.

Work Background
Continuing with MC, knit 6 rows, ending with
a WS row.

Continue to Make a Flap, Attach the Flap, and Work
Background until there are 38 Flaps or Scarf measures
approximately 44". End Scarf immediately after
attaching last Flap.

With A, BO all sts. Weave in ends from Flaps.

ATTACHING FLAPS TO BACKGROUND

1.

2.

Fringe

Of all the scarves in this book, Fringe is undoubtedly the easiest to knit. The only challenge a beginner might have is working with two strands of yarn held together and that's simple to do. Instructions are given for both three-color (see left) and four-color (see page 47) variations, but you can easily adapt them to as many colors as you like. Making this scarf is a great way to use yarn leftover from other projects.

||||||||||||||||||||||||||||

5" wide x 45" long

Manos del Uruguay Kettle-Dyed Wool
(100% wool; 138 yards / 100 grams): 4-
Color Scarf: 1 hank each #14 Natural (A),
#31 Nickel (B), #59 Kohl (C), and #08
Black (D); 3-Color Scarf: 1 hank each
#69 Hibiscus (A), #O Rose (B), and #14
Natural (C)

NEEDLES
One pair short single-pointed needles size
US 11 (8 mm)
Change needle size if necessary to obtain
correct gauge.

GAUGE
11 sts = 4" (10 cm) in Garter stitch
(knit every row), with 2 strands of yarn
held together

4-Color Scarf

With 2 strands of A held together, CO 15 sts,
leaving 4½" tails, and knit 2 rows.

Cut only one strand of A, leaving a tail the width
of the Scarf (see Photo 1).

Add one strand of B, matching the tail to the
width of the Scarf (see Photo 2).

*Note: Throughout the Scarf, when you cut a strand
or add a strand of yarn, match the length of the
tail to the width of the Scarf. These tails, plus the ones
from the CO and BO, are the fringe of the Scarf.*

Continue the Scarf, working the following
combinations in sequence.

* **STEP 1:** Knit 4 rows with 1 strand of A and
1 strand of B held together.

STEP 2: Knit 4 rows with 2 strands of B
held together.

STEP 3: Knit 4 rows with 1 strand of B and
1 strand of C held together.

STEP 4: Knit 4 rows with 2 strands of C
held together.

STEP 5: Knit 4 rows with 1 strand of C and
1 strand of D held together.

STEP 6: Knit 4 rows with 2 strands of D
held together.

Work back through the above combinations in
reverse, beginning with step 5 and ending with step 1.
Work 4 rows with 2 strands of A *. Repeat from * to *
2 more times.

BO all sts. Do NOT weave in ends; trim ends if
necessary to even them up.

3-Color Scarf

The same directions for adding and cutting yarns
for the 4-Color Scarf apply to the 3-Color Scarf.

With 2 strands of A held together, CO 15 sts,
leaving 4½" tails. Knit 8 rows.

*Begin the pattern sequence as for the 4-Color
Scarf, working steps 1-4 only, working from the
darkest color to the lightest. When you get to
the lightest solid-color section (Step 4), reverse the
sequence, beginning with step 3, until you are
back to 2 strands of the darkest color held together.

Knit 6 rows with 2 strands of A *. Repeat from * to *
until the Scarf is the desired length, ending with the
darkest color.

CUTTING YARN FOR FRINGE
AS YOU WORK

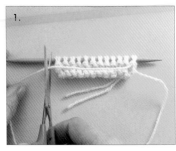

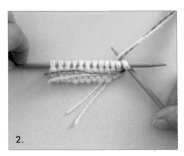

HOURGLASS

Much colorwork in knitting has a clear right and wrong side, but this two-color hourglass-shaped scarf is reversible, and can be tossed casually around the neck without any concern about which side is facing front. The single-color ribbed sections and the neck area are knit flat while the contrasting two-color slipstitch sections are knit around.

Finished Measurements
5" wide x 50" long

Yarn
Koigu Kersti (100% merino wool; 114 yards /
50 grams): 3 hanks #2239 (MC)
Koigu Premium Merino (KPM) (100%
merino wool; 170 yards / 50 grams):
1 hank #2220 (A)

Needles
One pair straight needles (SPN)
size US 11 (8 mm)
One set of three double-pointed
needles (DPN) size US 8 (5 mm)
Change needle size if necessary to
obtain correct gauge.

Gauge
13 sts = 4" (10 cm) in Stockinette stitch (St st)
using size 11 needles and 2 strands of MC
held together.

Techniques
Combine Stitches (see page 129)
Rib Division (see page 130)
Slip Stitch, Multicolor Patterns
  (see page 134)
Knitting Around on Two Double-Pointed
  Needles (see page 137)

Hourglass Chart
Work 12-st pattern twice around each rnd.

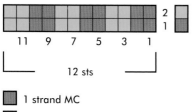

11 9 7 5 3 1

2
1

12 sts

▨ 1 strand MC
▢ 2 strands A held together

Note: For a full explanation of how to read slip
stitch charts, see page 134.

Text explanation of chart:
Rnd 1: With single strand of MC, [K2, Slip 2]
around all 24 sts on both needles.
Rnd 2: With 2 strands of A held together,
[Slip 2, K2] around all 24 sts on both sides.

Using larger needle and 2 strands of MC held
together, CO 24 sts.

Pattern
STEP 1:   With larger needles and 2 strands of MC
           held together, work in K2, P2 rib, slipping
           first K st of each row knitwise, until piece
           measures 3".

STEP 2:   Change to DPN and work one more
           row of rib. Divide sts onto two DPNs
           (see Rib Division, page 130). With 1 strand
           of MC, knit around all sts on both DPNs
           (see Knitting Around on Two Double-
           Pointed Needles, page 137).

STEP 3:   Begin Hourglass Chart, changing colors
           after every rnd as indicated. Work the 2 rnds
           of Chart five times.

STEP 4:   With 1 strand of MC, knit 2 rnds.

STEP 5:   With 2 strands of MC and DPN, Combine
           Stitches from both needles back into a
           K2, P2 rib (see page 129).

Repeat Pattern 2 more times, but on the final repeat,
increase 4 sts on the second rnd of Step 4, as follows:
[K3, LLI, knit to last 3 sts on needle, RLI, K3] on
each needle [28 sts; 14 sts each needle], then work
Step 5 to finish Pattern.

Change to larger needles and with the 2 strands of
MC held together, work K2, P2 rib for 15", slipping
first K st of each row knitwise.

Change to smaller needles and work 1 row K2, P2 rib.

Divide sts onto two DPNs. With 1 strand of MC,
knit around both needles, decrease 4 sts as follows:
[K3, K2tog, knit to last 5 sts on needle, K2tog, K3]
on each needle [24 sts remain; 12 sts each needle].

Work Pattern 3 times, beginning the first time
with Step 3.

Finish Scarf with 3" of K2, P2 rib to match the other
end of the Scarf. BO all sts in K2, P2 rib.

LABYRINTH

The inspiration for Labyrinth was the famed
Chanel jacket, first created in the 1920s.
Every time this popular classic comes back into
vogue, it seems to have ever more decorative
treatments on every visible edge. I used
the technique of Scrap Yarn Slits in this scarf
to create dozens of edges and then simply
bound off at each edge with a contrasting color
for decoration. This is an easy scarf to make,
and is a good choice for knitters just learning
to knit around.

Finished Measurements
4" wide x 54" long

Yarn
Queensland Collection Kathmandu Aran
(85% merino wool / 10% silk / 5% cashmere;
104 yards / 50 grams): 2 balls #145
Geranium (MC); 1 ball #135 Natural (A)
15 yards lighter weight contrasting color
scrap yarn (to be removed and discarded
when you work Decorative Edging)

Needles
One set of four double-pointed needles (DPN)
size US 10 (6 mm)
One pair double-pointed needles size
US 9 (5.5 mm) or smaller, for opening Scrap
Yarn Slits
Change needle size if necessary to obtain
correct gauge.

Notions
Stitch marker

Gauge
14 sts = 4" (10 cm) in Stockinette stitch (St st)

Techniques
Knitting Around (see page 136)
Scrap Yarn Slits (see page 138)

With MC and larger needles, CO 28 sts. Divide
stitches onto three DPNs [14, 7, and 7 sts]. Join for
working around, being careful not to twist sts; place
marker for beg of rnd. Knit 5 rnds.

Pattern
RND 1: Needle 1 [14 sts] - K1, Setup SYS
across 12 sts (see Scrap Yarn Slits, page 138), K1;
Needles 2 and 3 [7 sts each] - Knit all sts.
RNDS 2-8: Knit sts on all three needles.

Repeat the above 8-rnd pattern until Scarf measures
54", ending with Rnd 6 on the last repeat. BO all sts.

Decorative Edging
Edging is worked continuously. Do not cut yarn
between Slits.

With smaller needles, open the first Slit at the
bottom of the Scarf (see Open Scrap Yarn Slits,
page 139).

With A and larger needles, BO 11 sts on the lower
needle knitwise [1 st remains on DPN].

Pick up and knit 1 st at left side edge of opening
and BO previous st (see Photo 1).

Pick up, knit, and BO 2 more sts consecutively at left
side opening. A total of 3 sts have been BO at side
edge of opening (see Photo 2).

BO 11 sts on the upper needle.

Pick up and knit 1 st almost halfway between Slits
(see Photo 3). BO previous st.

Pick up, knit, and BO 1 more st at right side
[1 st remains on DPN to begin BO of next Slit]
(see Photo 4).

Open next Slit and work Decorative Edging around
it as for the previous Slit. Continue opening Slits
and working Decorative Edging until all Slits have
been finished.

WORKING DECORATIVE EDGING

LINKED RIB

You may be surprised to find out that this scarf is a variation of Tricorner (see page 108) because the two scarves look very different. Both use the same techniques of Rib Division (separating the knits from the purls on two different needles and working them separately) and Combine Stitches (putting those same stitches back onto one needle later). However, for Linked Rib, stitches are combined into flanges offset by five stitches from the previous flange; for Tricorner they are always lined up to match the previous flange. The unconventional way of working ribbing in rounds may seem challenging because of its novelty: You knit in and out on flanges instead of knitting an open circular tube. But I think you'll find it's easy once you review the instructional photos on page 59 and get started.

YARN
Rowan Yarns Summer Tweed (70% silk / 30% cotton; 118 yards / 50 grams):
2 hanks #540 Orient

NEEDLES
One set of six double-pointed needles (DPN) size US 8 (5 mm)
Change needle size if necessary to obtain correct gauge.

NOTIONS
Stitch markers

GAUGE
16 sts = 4" (10 cm) in Stockinette stitch (St st)

TECHNIQUES
Combine Stitches (see page 129)
Rib Division (see page 130)
Knitting Around (see page 136)

CO 30 sts loosely.

Set up Scarf Flanges
Slip first 5 sts onto an empty needle.
Slip the next 5 sts onto another empty needle.

Fold the second needle and hold parallel behind the first needle (see Photo 1).

With an empty needle, K1 from front needle and P1 from back needle (see Combine Stitches, page 129) until all 10 sts are worked in a K1, P1 rib onto one needle.

With an empty needle, rib the same 10 sts again, slipping first stitch knitwise.

Slip next 5 sts onto an empty needle and the following 5 sts onto another empty needle. Fold the second needle so it is behind and parallel to the first needle. With the working needle, K1 from the front needle and P1 from the back needle until all 10 sts are worked in a K1, P1 rib. With an empty needle, rib the same 10 sts again, slipping the first stitch knitwise. Repeat from * to * for the remaining 10 sts.

With working needle, rib the 10 sts of the first Flange, placing a marker 2 sts from the outside edge. Your knitting should look like Photo 2.

Work 3 rnds of Rib a Round (see right), then begin Scarf Pattern.

SCARF PATTERN
STEP 1: Divide Rib Flanges (see page 60).
STEP 2: Knit 5 rnds.
STEP 3: Combine Stitches Into Ribbed Flanges (see page 60).
STEP 4: Work 3 rnds of Rib a Round.

Repeat the four steps of Scarf Pattern until Scarf measures 60", ending with 3 rnds of Rib a Round.

To finish the Scarf, BO knitwise as you work Divide Rib Flanges.

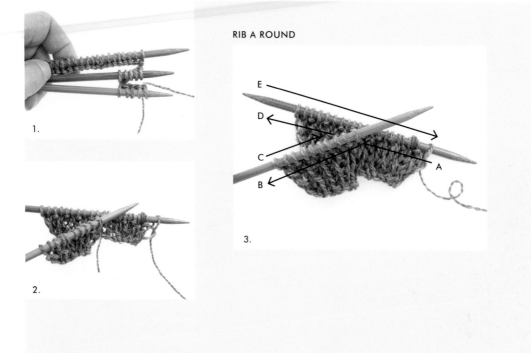

1.

2.

RIB A ROUND

3.

RIB A ROUND

Steps A–E below correspond to the letters in Photo 3. Before you begin knitting, read through the steps and see how the diagram corresponds to your knitting. Note that each round actually increases your Scarf by 2 rows:

A. With empty needle, K1, P1 for 10 sts, slipping first st knitwise.

B. With working needle, K1, P1 for next 10 sts, ending at outside edge of Flange.

C. With empty needle, K1, P1 for 10 sts (the same 10 sts worked in Step B), slipping first st knitwise.

D. With working needle, K1, P1 for next 10 sts, ending at outside edge of next Flange.

E. With empty needle, K1, P1 for 10 sts (the same 10 sts worked in Step D), slipping first st knitwise. Continue ribbing with working needle until you reach the outside edge of the Flange with the marker.

Divide Rib Flanges

Divide first 10 sts of needle with marker (see Rib Division, page 130). Slip marker to the back needle after the first purl st (see Photo 4).

With an empty needle, K5 sts on front (unmarked) working needle.

Divide the 10 sts on next needle. With working needle, knit next 5 sts on front needle of rib division. With an empty needle, knit next 5 sts from back needle of rib division.

Divide remaining 10 sts. Knit next 5 sts on front needle of rib division with working needle. With empty needle, knit next 10 sts, ending at the outside edge of the needle with marker (see Photo 5), which is the configuration for working Step 2 of Scarf Pattern.

4.

5.

Combine Stitches into Ribbed Flanges
(see Combine Stitches, page 129)

A. Divide the needle following the needle with marker into 5 sts each on 2 needles. Fold the second needle with 5 sts clockwise behind the first needle with 5 sts and hold them parallel together (see Photo 6).

B. With the working needle, combine the 2 parallel needles into a K1, P1 rib (see Photo 7).

C. With an empty needle, work the same 10 sts again in K1, P1 rib, slipping the first stitch knitwise. This completes the first Flange (see Photo 8).

Repeat directions for Steps A–C for the next two needles (photos do not represent work on repeats).

6.

7.

8.

MEANDERING STRIPES

I awoke from a dream one night with the
Cole Porter song "Fascinating Rhythm" in my
head, and this scarf is the graphic interpretation
that developed from the dream. I created
the gentle curves in this scarf with short rows.
It is shown at left in a soft combination of
apricot and natural and on page 65 in bolder
natural and slate.

Finished Measurements

5" wide x 58" long

Yarn

The Fibre Company Savannah (50% merino wool / 20% organic cotton / 15% linen / 15% soya; 65 yards / 50 grams): 2 hanks each Natural (A) and Slate or Apricot (B)

Needles and Notions

One pair short straight needles size US 10 (6 mm) Change needle size if necessary to obtain correct gauge.
Tapestry needle

Gauge

15 sts = 4" (10 cm) in Garter stitch (knit every row)

Technique

Working Short Rows in Garter Stitch (see page 140)

Note

The Scarf is made up of alternating Right and Left Curve sections. Each Curve section is made up of 3 Wedges. The wedge shape is created with the use of the Short Row Shaping technique.

Using A, CO 19 sts.

Work a Right Curve

Using A, follow directions for Right Wedge once.

Right Wedge

ROW 1 (RS): Knit all 19 sts.
ROWS 2 AND 3: Repeat Row 1.
ROW 4: Slip first st knitwise, knit remaining sts.
ROW 5: K17, W&T.
ROW 6: K17.
ROW 7: K15, W&T.
ROW 8: K15.
ROW 9: K13, W&T.
ROW 10: K13.
ROW 11: K11, W&T.
ROW 12: K11.
ROW 13: K9, W&T.
ROW 14: K9.
ROW 15: K7, W&T.
ROW 16: K7.
ROW 17: K5, W&T.
ROW 18: K5.
ROW 19: K3, W&T.
ROW 20: K3.

ROW 21: K1, W&T.
ROW 22: K1.
ROWS 23-25: Knit all 19 sts. *Note: It is not necessary to hide the wraps on Row 23 because they are sufficiently hidden by this yarn when worked in Garter stitch.*
Row 26: Slip first st knitwise, knit remaining sts.

Change to B and work Right Wedge once. Change back to A and work Right Wedge once.

Work a Left Curve

With B, follow directions for Left Wedge once.

Left Wedge

ROW 1 (RS): Knit all 19 sts.
ROW 2: Repeat Row 1.
ROW 3: Slip first st knitwise, knit remaining sts.
ROW 4: Knit all 19 sts.
ROW 5: Repeat Row 3.
ROW 6: K17, W&T.
ROW 7: K17.
ROW 8: K15, W&T.
ROW 9: K15.
ROW 10: K13, W&T.
ROW 11: K13.
ROW 12: K11, W&T.
ROW 13: K11.
ROW 14: K9, W&T.
ROW 15: K9.
ROW 16: K7, W&T.
ROW 17: K7.
ROW 18: K5, W&T.
ROW 19: K5.
ROW 20: K3, W&T.
ROW 21: K3.
ROW 22: K1, W&T.
ROW 23: K1.
ROW 24: Knit all 19 sts. *It is not necessary to hide the wraps with this yarn.*
ROW 25: Slip first st knitwise, knit remaining sts.
ROW 26: Repeat Row 24.

Change to A and work Left Wedge once. Change back to B and work Left Wedge once.

Continue to alternate Work a Right Curve (3 Right Wedges) and Work a Left Curve (3 Left Wedges) until you have a total of 8 Curves (24 Wedges). Weave in ends from the color changes to complete the Scarf.

New Wave

Smooth wave patterns are found everywhere –
in nature's rippling water, in man-made architectural
forms, and even in once-fashionable crimped
hair – but a three-dimensional wave pattern knit into
a scarf is undoubtedly new. The simple techniques
of Rib Division (separating the knits from the
purls on two different needles and working them
separately) and Combine Stitches (putting those
same stitches back onto one needle later)
allow you to knit uneven lengths around the scarf
and then lock sections in place to create the
wave shapes. Once you get started, the pattern
is a simple series of repeats.

Finished Measurements
4" wide x 52" long

Yarn
Harrisville Designs New England Knitters
Highland (100% pure wool, washed; 200 yards /
100 grams): 2 hanks #66 Melon
*Note: Harrisville also sells an unwashed version
of this yarn on cones. If you make the scarf
with the unwashed yarn, then wash the scarf without
agitating, the scarf will full and have an interesting
tighter wave (it may also shrink in length slightly).*

Needles
One set of three double-pointed needles (DPN)
size US 7 (4.5 mm)
One pair double-pointed needles size US 10 (6 mm)
Change needle size if necessary to obtain
correct gauge.

Gauge
12 sts = 4" (10 cm) in Stockinette stitch (St st) using
larger needles

Techniques
Combine Stitches (see page 129)
Rib Division (see page 130)
Knitting Around (see page 136)

With smaller needles, CO 28 sts and rib in K1, P1
for 2 rows, slipping first K st of each row knitwise.

Wave Pattern
Divide rib onto two needles (see Rib Division, page
130), place knit sts onto smaller needle held in front
and purl sts onto larger needle held in back. Divide
the sts on the smaller needle evenly onto two needles.

For the next 5 rnds, knit all sts on the smaller needles
with a smaller needle, and all sts on the larger needle
with a larger needle. Join for working around.

RND 1: Slip first st on first small needle knitwise.
Knit remaining sts on all needles.

RND 2: Knit all sts on all needles.

RND 3: Knit all sts on all needles. Keep larger needle
in front and slip edge st from smaller needle on
the left side to an empty needle.

Bring yarn between the slipped st and next st on
smaller needle, then slip st back onto smaller needle
(see Photo 1).

Turn work so that the smaller needles are in front.
Purl all 14 sts on larger needle. Turn work so larger
needle is in front.

Slip edge st from smaller needle on the right
side to the empty needle.

Bring yarn between slipped st and edge st
on smaller needle. Slip st back onto smaller needle
(see Photo 2).
Knit all sts on larger needle (end of Rnd 3).

RND 4: Hide wrap on first st of first smaller needle,
by knitting the wrap and st together.
Knit up to the last st on the second smaller needle.
Hide wrap on last st by knitting the
wrap and st together. Knit sts on larger needle.

RND 5: Knit all sts on all needles.

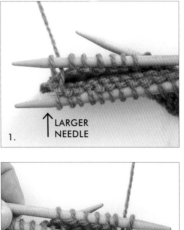

1. ↑ LARGER NEEDLE

2. LARGER NEEDLE ↑

Place all sts of both smaller needles onto one needle. With smaller needle held in front of larger needle, combine sts from both needles into a K1, P1 rib, using a smaller needle (see Combine Stitches, page 129). (*Note: Wave Pattern ends here.*)

Repeat Wave Pattern until Scarf measures 51½", ending with Rnd 4. *Note: When you begin a repeat and divide the rib sts, the front smaller needles hold the sts previously knit with the larger needles. The larger needle holds the sts previously knit with the smaller needles.*

On Rnd 5 of the final pattern repeat, decrease 1 st on first small needle, 2 sts across the second small needle, and 3 sts across the larger needle [22 sts remain]. Finish Wave Pattern.

Work one more row of rib. BO all sts tightly in K1, P1 rib.

Parallelograms

In homage to Josef Albers, a painter who based his entire body of work on his theories of color perception, I offer the Parallelograms scarf. Rather than the squares that Albers is known for, I used parallelograms and Garter ridges to blend two colors of yarn to create what appears to be a third color. Knitting this scarf doesn't require any special techniques, just knit, purl, increase, and decrease, and once you get started, you may find you don't even need to refer to the pattern.

YARN
Green Mountain Spinnery Mountain Mohair
(70% wool / 30% mohair; 140 yards /
2 ounces): 1 hank each Elderberry (A) and
Partridgeberry (B)

NEEDLES
One pair short straight needles size
US 10 (6 mm)
Change needle size if necessary to obtain
correct gauge.

GAUGE
15 sts = 4" (10 cm) in Stockinette
stitch (St st)

Using A, CO 20 sts. Change to B; leave A attached.

Scarf Pattern
Work Striped Garter, followed by Solid Stockinette.

STRIPED GARTER
ROW 1 (RS): Knit.

ROW 2 (WS): K1-f/b, knit to last 2 sts, K2tog.
Change color, and repeat Rows 1 and 2. When you
change colors, pick up the new color from behind.

Continue working Rows 1 and 2, alternating colors,
until there are 8 ridges (including the CO row),
ending with a WS Row. Cut the yarn used to knit the
last ridge, leaving a 3-4" tail.

SOLID STOCKINETTE
Work this section with the remaining attached yarn.
Work 6 rows of St st, ending with a WS row. After
the first row, slip the first stitch knitwise on knit
rows and purlwise on purl rows.

For the remainder of the piece repeat Scarf Pattern,
beginning the Striped Garter section with the
unattached color that was last cut off. Leave a 3-4"
tail when you reattach the yarn.

Knit until Scarf measures approximately 70" ending
with Striped Garter.

BO all stitches on the WS Row of the final
Garter ridge. Weave in ends. Lightly press WS of
scarf with a damp cloth and steam iron. Do not
flatten the Garter st.

Peek

For this achromatic scarf worked in Intarsia, white stitches peek out of "windows" in a light and dark gray fabric (see front view at left and back view on page 77). If you're new to Intarsia and would like to use the alpaca recommended in the pattern for the scarf, I suggest swatching with some scrap yarn first. The alpaca shown here is wonderful but it doesn't weather ripping out well, so isn't the best choice when you are first learning.

Finished Measurements
6" wide x 70" long

Yarn
Karabella Yarns Brushed Alpaca (100% alpaca; 35 yards / 50 grams): 1 ball each #71 Dark Gray (A), #77 Off White (B), and #51 Light Gray (C)

Needles
One pair straight needles size US 15 (10 mm)
One double-pointed needle (DPN) size US 15 (10 mm)
Note: You may use all DPNs if you prefer. Change needle size if necessary to obtain correct gauge.

Gauge
7 sts = 4" (10 cm) in Stockinette stitch (St st)

Technique
Intarsia Knitting (see page 132)

CO 4 sts each in A, B, and C [12 sts]. Work in St st for 6 rows, connecting the 3 colors with the Intarsia technique (see page 132). You should end with a WS row.

Follow instructions for Pattern.

Pattern
(RS) K4 in A. Slip next 4 sts (B) onto the DPN and hold in back. K4 in C, connecting them to the 4 sts in A with the Intarsia technique.

Work 5 more Intarsia rows with A and C, ending with a WS row.

Work 6 rows of B separately, ending with a WS row.

(RS) K4 in A, K4 in B from DPN, K4 in C, reconnecting all 3 colors with Intarsia.

Work 5 more rows of Intarsia with all 3 colors. *(Note: Pattern ends here.)*

Repeat Pattern 10 times.

Bind-Off
To maintain the appearance of vertical lines in the pattern, BO the Scarf as follows: BO A sts until 1 st of A remains on LH needle. BO remaining A st with B. BO B sts until 1 st of B remains on LH needle. BO remaining sts with C.

REVERSIBLE

Reversible is a simple, modernistic design that can be worn with either of its two colors on top. At first glance it appears to be unbalanced and asymmetrical, two-thirds of the scarf appearing to be just a single color. But the outline of the scarf does indeed have a symmetry, with identically shaped panels of the two colors overlapping to form mirrored collar lapels left and right.

Finished Measurements

6" wide (increasing to 9" at lower edge of collar) x 66" long

Yarn

Rowan Yarns Scottish Tweed Chunky (100% pure new wool; 109 yards / 100 grams): 1 ball each #17 Lobster (A) and #23 Midnight (B)

Needles

One pair straight needles size US 11 (8 mm) Change needle size if necessary to obtain correct gauge.

Notions

Tapestry needle

Gauge

11 sts = 4" (10 cm) in Garter stitch (knit every row)

Techniques

Intarsia Knitting (see page 132)
Short Row Shaping (see page 140)

Work entire Scarf in Garter st (knit every row).
Using A, CO 16 sts.
Knit for 18", ending with a WS row.

Next Row (RS): K14, K1-f/b, K1 [17 sts].
With the empty needle and B, CO 24 sts.
With needle holding A sts, connecting sts using the Intarsia Knitting technique (see page 132) and crossing yarns on the WS, knit across 24 sts CO in B [41 sts: 17 sts in A; 24 sts in B].
Continue working the two colors in Intarsia for 5 rows.

Decrease Row (RS): Work to 2 sts after Intarsia connection, K2tog [40 sts remain: 17 sts in A; 23 sts in B].

Repeat Decrease Row every 6 rows 6 more times [34 sts remain: 17 sts in A; 17 sts in B].

Continue working the two colors in Intarsia until B section measures 8" long, ending with a WS row. Begin Short Row Shaping (see page 140).

Begin Short Row Shaping

ROW 1 (RS): Continuing in A only, K15, W&T.
ROW 2: K15.
ROW 3: K10, W&T.
ROW 4: K10.
ROW 5: K5, W&T.
ROW 6: K5.
ROW 7: K17, hiding wraps, K17 in B.
ROW 8 (WS): Continuing in B only, K15, W&T.
ROW 9: K15.
ROW 10: K10, W&T.
ROW 11: K10.
ROW 12: K5, W&T.
ROW 13: K5.
ROW 14: K17, hiding wraps, K17 in A.

Continue knitting both colors in Intarsia and repeat Short Row Shaping every 6 rows 6 times.

Increase Row (RS): Work to 2 sts before Intarsia connection, K1-f/b [35 sts: 18 sts in A; 17 sts in B]. Repeat Increase Row every 6 rows 6 more times [41 sts: 24 sts in A; 17 sts in B].

Work for 5 more rows, ending with a WS row.
BO 24 sts (A), change to B, K1, K2tog, K14 [16 sts remain in B].

Continuing in B, work in Garter st for 18".
BO all sts. Weave in ends. Fold scarf lengthwise along Intarsia line.

SHAG

This is a three-dimensional scarf with triangle-
shaped flaps knitted at alternating angles.
All this texture and shape, without ever needing
to cut your yarn: Surpisingly to some knitters,
Shag is knit with one continuous strand.

FINISHED MEASUREMENTS
3" wide x 50" long

YARN
Alchemy Yarns Wabi Sabi (66% silk / 34%
wool; 86 yards / 50 grams): 2 hanks #069F
Kai's Goldfish

NEEDLES
One pair double-pointed or short straight
needles size US 9 (5.5 mm)
Change needle size if necessary to obtain
correct gauge.

GAUGE
16 sts = 4" (10 cm) in Garter stitch
(knit every row)

CO 13 sts.

PATTERN

STEP 1: Work in Garter stitch for 17 rows, slipping first
st of every row knitwise after first row. BO all but
last st. When working Step 1 for first time only, mark
lower left-hand corner with a piece of scrap yarn to
indicate WS (see Photo 1).

STEP 2: On WS, with attached yarn, pick up and knit
12 sts on the diagonal, starting at upper left-hand
corner and ending at bottom right-hand corner
(see Photo 2) [13 sts].

*Note: When you pick up sts on the diagonal the first time,
you will notice the flaps are offset (see Photo 3). This
is not a mistake. It is because the 13 sts by 17 rows form
a rectangle (not a square).*

STEP 3: Repeat Step 1.

STEP 4: On WS, with attached yarn, pick up and
knit 12 sts on the diagonal, starting at upper right-
hand corner and ending at bottom left-hand
corner [13 sts].

Repeat Pattern (steps 1-4) until Scarf measures about
49". To end Scarf, knit 3 rows after diagonal sts are
picked up. Then K2tog at beginning and end of every
other row until 3 sts remain. Knit last 3 sts together,
cut yarn, and pull through last st to fasten off.

BEGINNING PATTERN

1.   2.   3.

SHAWL COLLAR

Most scarves can be thrown on and wrapped around without any thought about their exact arrangement. This is the only scarf in the book that needs to be worn in a specific way, that is if you want to achieve the shawl collar look as shown at left. To see another way to wear it, see page 89. If you want the rib to hold its shape, I suggest you read "A Few Words About Ribs" on page 8.

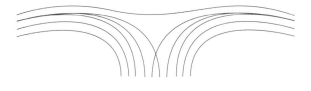

Finished Measurements

6" wide x 21" or 27" long from center back
Note: Shown 21" long on page 86 and 27" long on page 89.

Yarn

Blue Sky Alpacas Dyed Cotton (100% organically grown cotton; 150 yards / 100 grams): 3 hanks #619 Tomato

Needles

One pair straight needles size US 9 (5.5 mm)
One 32" (82 cm) circular needle size US 9 (5.5 mm)
Change needle size if necessary to obtain correct gauge.

Gauge

16 sts = 4" (10 cm) in Stockinette stitch (St st)

Technique

Short Row Shaping (see page 140)

Note

To keep your ribbing from spreading, when carrying yarn between needles, add some tension to keep the yarn from becoming slack. Do not work tight stitches, as that will make it difficult to keep your gauge consistent.

Work Left Side instructions, followed by Right Side instructions. They will be connected when you work the Collar.

Left Side

CO 42 sts. Work in K3, P3 rib, slipping first K st of each row knitwise, until piece measures 16 (22)".
Continuing in K3, P3, slipping first K st of each odd-numbered row knitwise, begin Short Row Shaping (see page 140):
ROW 1 (RS): Rib 38 sts, W&T.
ROW 2: Rib 38 sts, beginning with P2.
ROW 3: Rib 36 sts, W&T.
ROW 4: Rib 36 sts.
ROW 5: Rib 32 sts, W&T.
ROW 6: Rib 32 sts, beginning with P2.
ROW 7: Rib 30 sts, W&T.
ROW 8: Rib 30 sts.
ROW 9: Rib 26 sts, W&T.
ROW 10: Rib 26 sts, beginning with P2.
ROW 11: Rib 24 sts, W&T.
ROW 12: Rib 24 sts.
ROW 13: Rib 20 sts, W&T.
ROW 14: Rib 20 sts, beginning with P2.
ROW 15: Rib 18 sts, W&T.
ROW 16: Rib 18 sts.
ROW 17: Rib 14 sts, W&T.
ROW 18: Rib 14 sts, beginning with P2.
ROW 19: Rib 12 sts, W&T.
ROW 20: Rib 12 sts.
ROW 21: Rib 8 sts, W&T.
ROW 22: Rib 8 sts, beginning with P2.
ROW 23: Rib 6 sts, W&T.
ROW 24: Rib 6 sts.
ROW 25: Rib all 42 sts, hiding the wraps as you knit.
Slip these sts onto the circular needle while you work the Right Side (knitting continues back and forth; circular needle used to accomodate all of the stitches for both sides later).

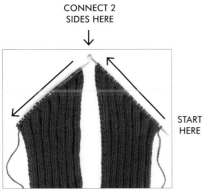

CONNECT 2
SIDES HERE
↓

START
HERE

BEGINNING COLLAR

RIGHT SIDE

Work as for Left Side, beginning Short-Row Shaping
on a WS row rather than a RS row.

COLLAR

To begin Collar, connect Left and Right
sides as follows:
With RS of Right Side piece facing you, rib 42 sts,
slipping first K st. Connect to Left Side (RS facing
and attached yarn at opposite end of where you
will begin knitting); rib all 42 sts of left side (do NOT
slip first st) (see Photo at left). Continue to work
the two connected sides in K3, P3 rib, slipping first
K st of each row, for 7". BO all sts in K3, P3 rib.

STACKED WEDGES

Alternating wedges in changing colors give
this scarf an undulating patchwork look.
It's a great unisex design that is made more
masculine or feminine by color choice. It is
shown in one- and four-color variations
but you can make it in up to thirteen colors,
one for each wedge for a kaleidoscopic
effect (and to effectively diminish an
overflowing yarn stash).

FINISHED MEASUREMENTS
5½" wide x 60" long

YARN
Harrisville Designs Flax & Wool Blend
(80% fine wool / 20% flax; 245 yards /
100 grams): 4-Color Version: 1 hank each
#222 Spice (A), #223 Fieldstone (B),
#225 Birch (C), and #224 Slate (D).
*Note: There is enough yarn in each hank
to work a second 4-color scarf, however,
the color arrangement will need to
be different since you will have used up
more of A and C than B and D.*
Solid-Color Version: 2 hanks #225 Birch

NEEDLES
One pair straight needles size
US 8 (5 mm)
Change needle size if necessary to
obtain correct gauge.

NOTIONS
Tapestry needle

GAUGE
16 sts = 4" (10 cm) in Garter stitch
(knit every row)

TECHNIQUE
Short Row Shaping (see page 140)

Four-Color Scarf
The Scarf is knit by alternating Right and Left Wedges.
The Wedges are shaped using Short Row Shaping
(see page 140).
The color sequence of the Wedges is *A, B, C, A, D,
C*; repeat from * to *.
With A, CO 21 sts.

RIGHT WEDGE
ROW 1 (RS): K21.
ROWS 2-4: Repeat Row 1.
ROW 5: K19, W&T.
ROW 6: K19.
ROW 7: K17, W&T.
ROW 8: K17.
ROW 9: K15, W&T.
ROW 10: K15.
ROW 11: K13, W&T.
ROW 12: K13.
ROW 13: K11, W&T.
ROW 14: K11.
ROW 15: K9, W&T.
ROW 16: K9.
ROW 17: K7, W&T.
ROW 18: K7.
ROW 19: K5, W&T.
ROW 20: K5.
ROW 21: K3, W&T.
ROW 22: K3.
ROW 23: K1, W&T.
ROW 24: K1.
ROW 25: K21, hiding wraps as you knit.
ROWS 26-28: K21.
With same color, repeat Rows 3-28 once.

Change to next color in sequence and work
Left Wedge.

LEFT WEDGE

ROW 1 (RS): K21.

ROWS 2–5: Repeat Row 1.

ROW 6: K19, W&T.

ROW 7: K19.

ROW 8: K17, W&T.

ROW 9: K17.

ROW 10: K15, W&T.

ROW 11: K15.

ROW 12: K13, W&T.

ROW 13: K13.

ROW 14: K11, W&T.

ROW 15: K11.

ROW 16: K9, W&T.

ROW 17: K9.

ROW 18: K7, W&T.

ROW 19: K7.

ROW 20: K5, W&T.

ROW 21: K5.

ROW 22: K3, W&T.

ROW 23: K3.

ROW 24: K1, W&T.

ROW 25: K1.

ROW 26: K21, hiding wraps as you knit.

ROWS 27–31: K21.

With same color, repeat Rows 6–28 once.

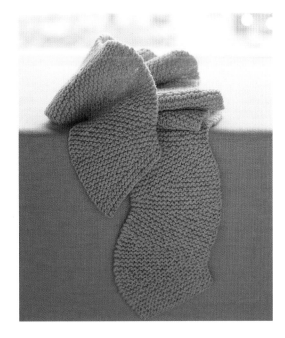

Continue to alternate Right and Left Wedges, changing to next color in sequence for each new Wedge. Work until piece measures 60" or you have completed 13 Wedges. BO all sts. Weave in the tails from the color changes and your Scarf is finished.

Solid-Color Scarf

Work the Scarf as for the 4-Color Version, but with one continuous solid-color yarn. There will be no tails from color changes to weave in.

STRIPED ILLUSION

While designing this scarf I revisited a color exercise I was assigned in a basic design course in college: to use dark and light stripes to create an optical illusion. Here, the alternating colored stripes are used to create larger shapes that appear to be layered on top of each other while in actuality they are flat.

FINISHED MEASUREMENTS
5½" wide x 56" long

YARN
Elsebeth Lavold Silky Wool (65% wool / 35% silk;
191 yards / 50 grams): 1 hank each #003 Granite
(A) and #001 Chalk (B)

NEEDLES
One pair short straight needles size US 5 (3.75 mm)
Change needle size if necessary to obtain
correct gauge.

GAUGE
23 sts = 4" (10 cm) in Garter stitch (knit every row)

TECHNIQUES
Add On Stitches (see page 128)
Intarsia Knitting (see page 132)

Using A, CO 19 sts.

Scarf begins with a RS row. Purl every row for 5
rows (end with a RS row).

Change to B and purl every row for 6 rows (end with
a RS row).

At the beginning of the next row, add on 11 sts with
B (see Add On Stitches, page 128).

Now, follow Striped Illusion Chart on page 98,
working color changes with the Intarsia technique
(see page 132) and increases and decreases as
indicated. When you complete Row 318 of the Chart,
begin again at Row 1 and work until Scarf is 56" or
desired length, finishing on a RS row with a complete
purl side stripe, and working knit side sts in the same
color as the previous knit side row.

BO all sts on the knit-only side. Continue using
color from knit side and work one more stripe on
purl-only side. BO all remaining sts.

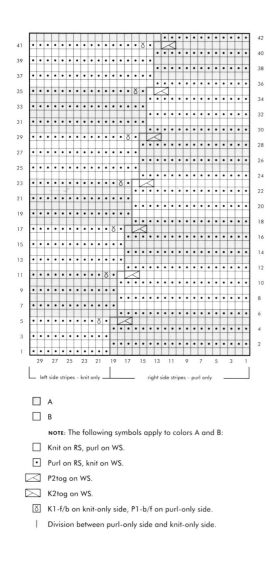

left side stripes – knit only | right side stripes – purl only

☐ A

☐ B

NOTE: The following symbols apply to colors A and B:

☐ Knit on RS, purl on WS.

▪ Purl on RS, knit on WS.

◺ P2tog on WS.

◹ K2tog on WS.

◰ K1-f/b on knit-only side, P1-b/f on purl-only side.

| Division between purl-only side and knit-only side.

HOW TO READ THE CHART

The Chart begins with a WS row; therefore you
will start the Chart on Row 1, at the left-hand side,
and work across from left to right on WS rows,
and from right to left on RS rows, as follows:

ROW 1 (WS): K11 in B, twist colors (Intarsia),
P19 in A.

ROW 2: P19 in A, twist colors (Intarsia), K11 in B.

Continue to follow the Chart, connecting
colors with the Intarsia technique, and working
increases and decreases as indicated.

All stripes on the left-hand side of the Chart are
knit every row. All stripes on the right-hand
side are purled every row. The change from purl
to knit is indicated by a solid red line.

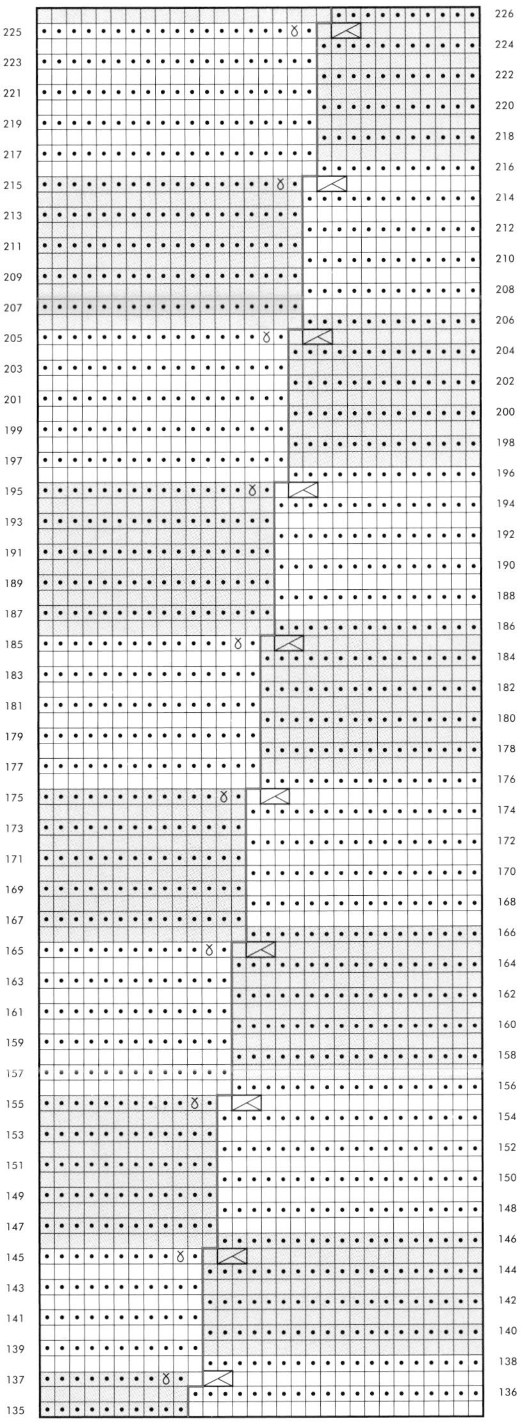
225 223 221 219 217 215 213 211 209 207 205 203 201 199 197 195 193 191 189 187 185 183 181 179 177 175 173 171 169 167 165 163 161 159 157 155 153 151 149 147 145 143 141 139 137 135
226 224 222 220 218 216 214 212 210 208 206 204 202 200 198 196 194 192 190 188 186 184 182 180 178 176 174 172 170 168 166 164 162 160 158 156 154 152 150 148 146 144 142 140 138 136

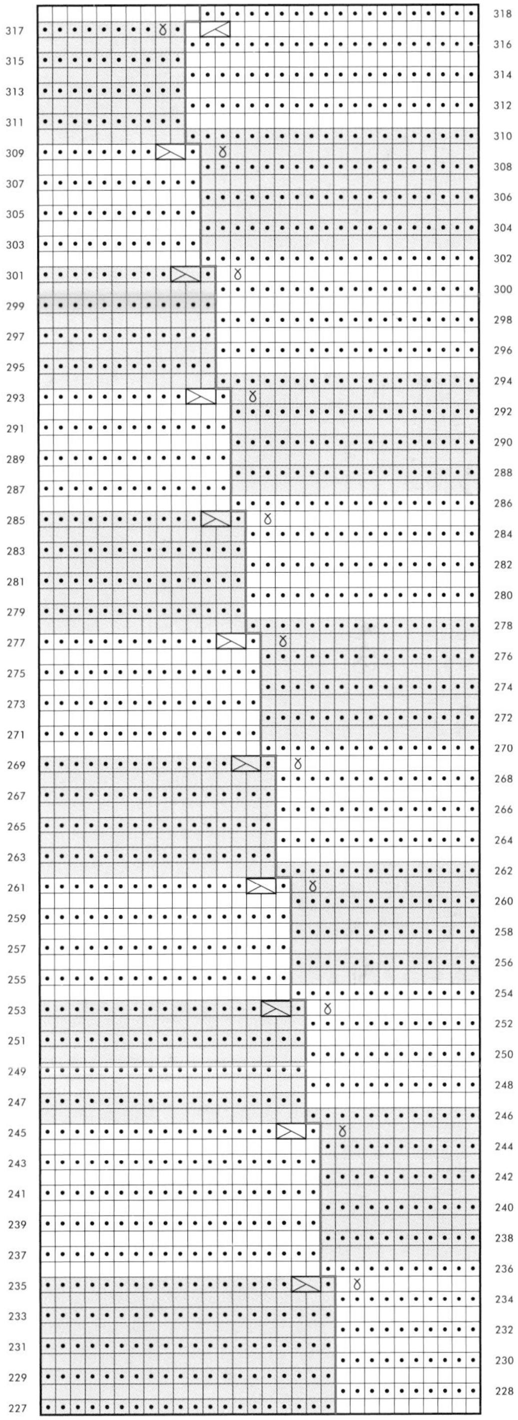
317 315 313 311 309 307 305 303 301 299 297 295 293 291 289 287 285 283 281 279 277 275 273 271 269 267 265 263 261 259 257 255 253 251 249 247 245 243 241 239 237 235 233 231 229 227
318 316 314 312 310 308 306 304 302 300 298 296 294 292 290 288 286 284 282 280 278 276 274 272 270 268 266 264 262 260 258 256 254 252 250 248 246 244 242 240 238 236 234 232 230 228

STRIPED WEDGES

The scarf has a simple, yet bold design. The wedges are created using easy Short Row Shaping, and because the scarf is knit from side edge to side edge with only four stripes of color, there are very few tails of yarn to weave in at the end.

FINISHED MEASUREMENTS
9" wide at widest point (3½" at narrowest
point) x 40" long

YARN
Peace Fleece Worsted Weight Knitting Yarn
(70% wool / 30% mohair; 200 yards /
4 ounces): 1 hank each Baku Black (A),
Negotiation Gray (B), Antarctica White (C),
and Fathers Gray (D)

NEEDLES
One 32" (82 cm) or longer circular needle
size US 9 (5.5 mm)
Change needle size if necessary to obtain
correct gauge.

NOTIONS
Tapestry needle

GAUGE
15 sts = 4" (10 cm) in Garter stitch
(knit every row)

TECHNIQUE
Short Row Shaping (see page 140)

Using A, CO 150 sts. The circular needle is
used for length; sts should NOT be connected
and knit around.

Scarf Pattern

Knit 2 rows, then begin Short Rows
(see Short Row Shaping, page 140).

SHORT ROWS
ROW 1: K11, W&T.
ROW 2: K11.
ROW 3: K22, hiding wrap, W&T.
ROW 4: K22.
ROW 5: K33, hiding wrap, W&T.
ROW 6: K33.
ROW 7: K44, hiding wrap, W&T.
ROW 8: K44.
ROW 9: K55, hiding wrap, W&T.
ROW 10: K55.
ROW 11: Knit across all 150 sts, hiding wrap.

Repeat Rows 1–11 for this end of Scarf.
(*Note: Scarf Pattern ends here.*)

Change to B, work Scarf Pattern again, and
knit 2 additional rows at the end of the pattern.

Change to C, work Scarf Pattern again, and
knit 2 additional rows at the end of the pattern.

Change to D, work Scarf Pattern and knit
1 additional row at the end of the pattern.

BO all sts. Weave in ends from color changes.

TILTED BLOCKS

This scarf is similar to a stairway my husband
and I designed for our house. The stairs are more
cantilevered than tilted, but both the stairs and
the scarf create an illusion of precarious instability
that I find intriguing. Tilted Blocks is easy to
knit and just requires the basic skills of bind-off,
add on, and a simple increase and decrease.

FINISHED MEASUREMENTS
5½" wide (blocks measured diagonally) x
60" long

YARN
Rowan Yarns Scottish Tweed Chunky (100%
pure new wool; 109 yards / 100 grams):
4-Color Version: 1 ball each #17 Lobster (A),
#23 Midnight (B), #07 Lewis Grey (C),
and #24 Porridge (D); Solid-Color Version:
2 balls #19 Peat

NEEDLES
One pair short straight needles size
US 10½ (6.5 mm)
Change needle size if necessary to obtain
correct gauge.

NOTIONS
Tapestry needle

GAUGE
12 sts = 4" (10 cm) in Garter stitch
(knit every row)

TECHNIQUE
Add On Stitches (see page 128)

4-Color Scarf

With color of your choice, CO 15 sts and begin
Garter st (knit every row). Work until there
are 12 ridges showing on the RS, including the
CO ridge. You will end with a WS row.

BEGIN NEW BLOCK

ROW 1 (RS): BO 3 sts. With the new block color, knit
1 st and BO remaining st of previous block color.
Cut the yarn from the previous block, leaving
a 3" tail. Continuing with yarn for the new block,
K1-f/b, knit to last 2 sts, K2tog [11 sts].

ROW 2: Add on 4 sts (see Add On Stitches, page 128).
Knit all 15 sts.

Continue working in Garter st until there are
12 ridges on the RS and you have just completed
a WS row.

*Note: Since two knit rows create one ridge, you will
knit a total of 24 rows for each block. The blocks
are not square and should be slightly larger in width
than in height.*

Repeat from Begin New Block with a different
color each time. Fourteen Blocks should make
a 60" Scarf. BO the final Block on the last WS row.
Weave in ends from color changes.

Solid-Color Scarf

Work the Blocks same as for the 4-Color Version,
but do NOT cut yarn between Blocks. When you
Begin a New Block, you will omit the color change
and will BO 4 sts on Row 1.

TRICORNER

Tricorner was my second and more successful attempt (after Twisted, see page 114) at capturing in knitting the shape of the Infinity Tower, a residential high-rise building in Dubai, United Arab Emirates, which "twists" ninety degrees over the course of its eighty-story rise. Knitting this scarf may seem difficult at first because of the unconventional way of knitting around, but I think you'll find it's easy once you take a look at the instructional photos included in the pattern and work a few rounds. Remember as a beginning knitter how complicated cables looked, but once you worked some you realized they were easy?

≫ ≫ ≫ ≫ ≫ ≫ ≫ ≫ ≫

Finished Measurements

3" wide x 54" long

Yarn

Classic Elite Yarns Allure (50% very fine merino /
25% cashmere / 25% angora; 110 yards /
50 grams): 2 hanks #10308 Coral

Needles

One set of six double-pointed needles (DPN) size
US 8 (5 mm)
Change needle size if necessary to obtain
correct gauge.

Notions

Stitch marker

Gauge

17 sts = 4" (10 cm) in Garter stitch (knit every row)

Techniques

Combine Stitches (see page 129)
Rib Division (see page 130)
Knitting Around (see page 136)

CO 30 sts.

Tricorner Setup

Slip first 5 sts onto an empty needle. Slip the next
5 sts onto another empty needle.

Fold the second needle so it is held parallel to and
behind the first needle (see Photo 1).

With an empty needle, K1 from front needle
and P1 from back needle (see Combine Stitches,
page 129) until all 10 sts are worked in a K1,
P1 rib onto one needle.

With an empty needle, work the 10 sts again in K1,
P1 pattern, slipping first K st of each row knitwise,
and placing a marker after the second st.

Repeat from the beginning of Tricorner Setup for
the next 20 sts, using the working needle to combine
sts, until the 30 sts are divided into three flanges
of 10 sts each. Do not place markers on the second
and third flanges.

With the working needle, rib to the outside edge of
the first flange with the marker. This is the completed
Tricorner Setup (see Photo 2).

TRICORNER SETUP

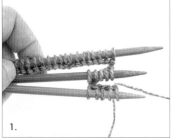

1.

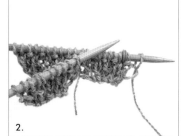

2.

BEGIN SCARF PATTERN
Work through the following 4 steps:

STEP 1: Rib 3 Tricorner Rounds
The beginning and end of a round should look like Photo 3. Steps A–E below correspond to the letters in Photo 3. Before you begin knitting, read through the steps and see how the diagram corresponds to your knitting:

A. With empty needle, K1, P1 for 10 sts, slipping first K st knitwise.
B. With working needle, K1, P1 on next 10 sts, ending at outside edge of flange.
C. With empty needle, K1, P1 for 10 sts (the same 10 sts ribbed in Step B), slipping first K st knitwise.
D. With working needle, K1, P1 on next 10 sts, ending at outside edge of next flange.
E. With empty needle, K1, P1 for 10 sts (the same 10 sts ribbed in Step D), slipping first K st knitwise. Continue ribbing with working needle until you reach the outside edge of the flange with the marker.

STEP 2: Change to conventional knitting-around setup as follows:

Divide 10-st rib of first flange (with marker) (see Rib Division, page 130). Slip marker to back needle with purl sts, placing it after the first purl st (see Photo 4).

Purl the 5 sts on the front needle with an empty needle.

Divide 10-st rib of next flange. Purl the 5 sts on the front needle with the working needle. Purl the next 5 sts with an empty needle.

Divide the 10-st rib of the last flange. Purl the front 5 sts with the working needle. With an empty needle purl the next 5 sts and the remaining 5 sts (with marker) from the first flange division (see Photo 5).

STEP 3: Work in Garter st (knit 1 rnd, purl 1 rnd), until there are 4 ridges, ending with a knit rnd.

STEP 4: Change to Tricorner Setup as follows: Divide the sts on the needle following the needle with the marker onto two needles with 5 sts each. Hold the needle with the marker parallel to and behind the next needle. With an empty needle, combine sts from both needles back into a 10-st flange, using K1, P1 rib and slipping marker after first purl st.

Divide the needle with 10 sts (opposite the working needle) onto two needles with 5 sts each. With the working needle, combine sts from the next two needles to create a 10-st ribbed flange. With an empty needle, rib the same 10 sts again, slipping first K st knitwise, to complete the second flange.

With the working needle, combine sts from the remaining two needles into the third 10-st flange. To complete the third flange, with an empty needle, rib the same 10 sts again, slipping first st knitwise.

With the working needle, rib to the outside edge of the first flange (with marker) to complete the Tricorner Setup. The arrangement of needles should once again look like Photo 3. (*Note: This is the end of Step 4.*)

Repeat the four steps of Scarf Pattern until scarf is approximately 54" long, ending with the rib section of Step 1.

BIND OFF SCARF

Divide rib of first flange. BO the 5 sts on front needle knitwise. Divide sts of next flange. BO the sts on the front needle, then the back needle, knitwise. Divide the last flange and BO all remaining sts knitwise, including the 5 sts remaining from the first flange.

STEP 1: TRICORNER ROUNDS

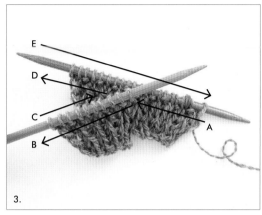

3.

STEP 2: CHANGE TO CONVENTIONAL KNITTING-AROUND SETUP

4.

5.

Twisted

This scarf is the outcome of my first attempt to create a knit version of the fascinating Infinity Tower in Dubai. Within five inches, I knew I'd missed my mark (see my second attempt on page 108), but I was still pleased with the shape. I narrowed it so it could wrap around without warping, and I lengthened it so it could wrap many times around a neck to keep its wearer warm. The finished scarf may look complex, but it's actually pretty simple to knit. Once you work through the pattern repeats a few times, you probably won't even need to refer to the pattern.

FINISHED MEASUREMENTS

Aran Version (page 114): 2½" wide x
110" long (enough to wrap three times
around neck)
Chunky Version (page 117): 3" wide x 85"
long (enough to wrap twice around neck)

YARN
Aran Version: Rowan Yarns Scottish Tweed
Aran (100% pure new wool; 186 yards /
100 grams): 2 balls #09 Rust
Chunky Version: Rowan Yarns Scottish
Tweed Chunky (100% pure new wool; 109
yards / 100 grams): 2 balls #13 Claret

NEEDLES
Aran Version: One set of three double-
pointed needles (DPN) size US 10 (6 mm)
Chunky Version: One set of three double-
pointed needles size US 10 ¾ (7 mm)
Change needle size if necessary to obtain
correct gauge.

GAUGE
Aran Version: 14 sts = 4" (10 cm) in
Stockinette stitch (St st) using smaller needles
and Aran Yarn
Chunky Version: 12 sts = 4" (10 cm)
Stockinette stitch (St st) using larger
needles and Chunky Yarn

TECHNIQUES
Combine Stitches (see page 129)
Rib Division (see page 130)
Knitting Around on Two Double-Pointed
   Needles (see page 137)

NOTE
Instructions are for both versions. Remember
to use the appropriate needle size for the
yarn used.

Using yarn of your choice and corresponding
needle size, CO 16 sts. Work in K1, P1 rib for 6 rows,
slipping first K st of each row knitwise.

Scarf Pattern

Divide sts onto two needles [8 sts on each needle]
(see Rib Division, page 130).

Slip first st on first needle knitwise (pull taut) and knit
around remaining sts on both needles (see Knitting
Around on Two Double-Pointed Needles, page 137).

Knit 4 more rounds, but do NOT slip first st.

BEGIN FOUR-STITCH SHIFT
Knit 4 sts on next needle [4 sts working needle, 4 sts
next needle, 8 sts previous needle] (see Photo below).
Combine sts in blue box in Photo onto one needle
by slipping 4 sts from previous needle onto back
end of working needle. Combine sts in red box onto
one needle by slipping 4 remaining sts from previous
needle onto back end of next needle [8 sts each on
two needles]. (Note: Four-Stitch Shift ends here.)

K1 from front needle and P1 from back needle until
all 16 sts are worked in a K1, P1 rib onto one needle
(see Combine Stitches, page 129).

Work in K1, P1 rib for 4 more rows, slipping first
K st of each row knitwise at beginning of each row.
(Note: Scarf Pattern ends here.)

Repeat Scarf Pattern until scarf measures
approximately 110" for Aran Version [85" for
Chunky Version]. BO all sts in K1, P1 rib.

Woven Cords

I came up with the idea for this scarf while playing
with some knitted I-cord—weaving it just seemed
a natural thing to do. In the scarf shown, four dark
gray warp cords are woven together with a single
lighter gray weft cord. The weaving part can
feel a bit unwieldy while you're doing it but once
all the cords are in place, clear elastic cord secures
it all together into a soft loose fabric. If you made
little potholders on a loom when you were a
kid, then you already understand the simple over
and under process of weaving.

Finished Measurements
4" wide x 60" long

Yarn
Peace Fleece Worsted Weight Knitting
Yarn (70% wool / 30% mohair; 200 yards /
4 ounces): 1 hank each Fathers Gray
(MC – for warp / vertical cords) and Negotiation
Gray (A – for weft / weaving cord)

Needles
One pair double-pointed needles (DPN)
size US 10½ (6.5 mm)
One pair double-pointed needles size
US 9 (5.5 mm)

Notions
Tapestry needle; 1 spool of .5mm clear
elastic cord (available in bead stores and in
craft stores that carry beading supplies)

Gauge
Gauge is unimportant for this scarf.

Technique
Knitting I-Cord (see page 135)

Knitting the Warp Cords
These are the vertical Cords.
Using larger needle and MC, CO 6 sts. Following
instructions for Knitting I-Cord (see page 135),
work until I-Cord measures 72". BO all sts.
Make 3 more Warp Cords [4 Cords].

Knitting the Weft Cord
This is the long Cord used to weave under and
over the Warp Cords.

Using smaller needle and A, CO 5 sts. Following
instructions for Knitting I-Cord, work until
I-Cord measures 200" [1 Cord]. BO all sts.

Weaving the Scarf
STEP 1: Lay the 4 Warp Cords parallel to each other
on a large flat surface (floor or table). Using
scrap yarn, temporarily baste the 4 Cords together
4" from the top.

STEP 2: Pull back Warp Cords 1 and 3 and lay the
Weft Cord across Warp Cords 2 and 4, starting
4" from beginning of Weft Cord and below
basting on Warp Cords.

STEP 3: Put Warp Cords 1 and 3 back down, and
pull back Warp Cords 2 and 4. Bring the Weft Cord
back across Warp Cords 1 and 3.

Weave by repeating steps 2 and 3 until you are 4" away
from the end of the Warp Cords.

STEP 4: When you have finished weaving, thread a
tapestry needle with the clear elastic cord. Lock the
weaving together by running the elastic through
all 4 Warp Cords, between each Weft crossing. The
elastic will be hidden inside the I-Cords. Remove
the scrap yarn.

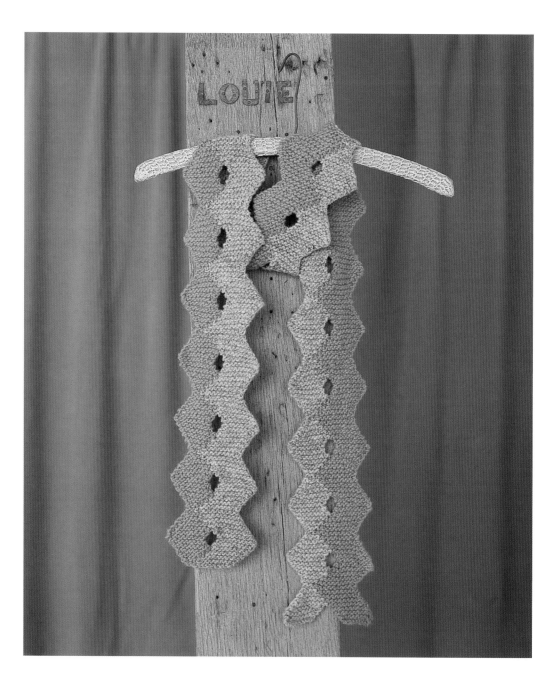

ZigZag

This scarf is an optical illusion, with one zigzag color seemingly hiding behind the other. It is created using the Intarsia technique. If you are new to Intarsia, you may want to practice with some scrap yarn first.

FINISHED MEASUREMENTS
4½" wide x 58" long

YARN
Green Mountain Spinnery Mountain Mohair
(70% wool / 30% mohair; 140 yards /
2 ounces): 1 hank each Day Lily (A) and
Blizzard (B) (see page 122) or Coral Bell (A)
and Alpine Shadow (B) (see page 125)

NEEDLES
One pair short straight needles size US 7
(4.5 mm)
Change needle size if necessary to obtain
correct gauge.

GAUGE
18 sts = 4" (10 cm) in Garter stitch (knit
every row)

TECHNIQUE
Intarsia Knitting (see page 132)

On one needle, CO 10 sts in B, then
10 sts in A [20 sts].

Work colors separately (do not use Intarsia)
for the following 7 rows:
ROW 1 (RS): Knit A sts. Knit B sts.
ROWS 2, 4, AND 6: Knit B sts. Knit A sts.
ROWS 3, 5, AND 7: With A, SSK, K7, K1-f/b.
With B, K1-f/b, K7, K2tog.

Work Rows 8–24 using the Intarsia technique
(see page 132). The directions will say "Twist"
when changing from one color to another.
Yarns are always twisted on the WS of the Scarf.
ROWS 8, 10, 12, 14, 16, 18, 20, 22, AND 24: Knit B sts;
Twist; Knit A sts.
ROW 9: With A, SSK, K9; Twist; with B, K7,
K2tog [18 sts remain].
ROW 11: With A, SSK, K9; Twist; with B, K5,
K2tog [16 sts remain].
ROW 13: With A, SSK, K9; Twist; with B, K3,
K2tog [14 sts remain].
ROW 15: With A, SSK, K9; Twist; with B, K1,
K2tog [12 sts remain].

ROW 17: With A, K1-f/b, K8; Twist; with B, K2,
K1-f/b [14 sts].
ROW 19: With A, K1-f/b, K8; Twist; with B, K4,
K1-f/b [16 sts].
ROW 21: With A, K1-f/b, K8; Twist; with B, K6,
K1-f/b [18 sts].
ROW 23: With A, K1-f/b, K8; Twist; with B, K8,
K1-f/b [20 sts].

Again, work colors separately and do not twist
for Rows 25–31.
ROWS 25 AND 27: With A, K1-f/b, K7, K2tog.
With B, SSK, K7, K1-f/b.
ROWS 26, 28, AND 30: Knit B sts. Knit A sts.
ROWS 29 AND 31: With A, SSK, K7, K1-f/b.
With B, K1-f/b, K7, K2tog.

Repeat Rows 8–31 nine times, and then move on
to the following section, beginning with Row 32.

Work Rows 32–48 using the Intarsia technique.
ROWS 32, 34, 36, 38, 40, 42, 44, 46, AND 48:
Knit B sts; Twist; Knit A sts.
ROW 33: With A, SSK, K7; Twist; with B, K9,
K2tog [18 sts remain].
ROW 35: With A, SSK, K5; Twist; with B, K9,
K2tog [16 sts remain].
ROW 37: With A, SSK, K3; Twist; with B, K9,
K2tog [14 sts remain].
ROW 39: With A, SSK, K1; Twist; with B, K9,
K2tog [12 sts remain].
ROW 41: With A, K1-f/b, K2; Twist; with B, K8,
K1-f/b [14 sts].
ROW 43: With A, K1-f/b, K4; Twist; with B, K8,
K1-f/b [16 sts].
ROW 45: With A, K1-f/b, K6; Twist; With B, K8,
K1-f/b [18 sts].
ROW 47: With A, K1-f/b, K8; Twist; With B, K8,
K1-f/b [20 sts].

Work colors separately and do not twist
for rows 49–55.
ROWS 49 AND 51: With A, K1-f/b, K7, K2tog.
With B, SSK, K7, K1-f/b.
ROWS 50, 52, AND 54: Knit B sts. Knit A sts.
ROWS 53 AND 55: With A, SSK, K7, K1-f/b.
With B, K1-f/b, K7, K2tog.

Repeat Rows 32–55 nine times. End the last repeat
on Row 39. BO B sts with B and A sts with A.

TECHNIQUES

Add On Stitches

This technique is used to add new stitches onto the edge of a work in progress. Unlike stitches added onto a garment that might be hidden in seams, these stitches will be visible.

There are a variety of ways to add on stitches: by knitting between the two edge stitches, by knitting into the edge stitch, or by the method presented in this book. Adding on a stitch using the first two methods leaves a hole between the work in progress and the first new stitch, but the method below creates a seamless connection.

STEP 1: Hold knitting in your left hand and working yarn in your right hand. Make a full twist-and-a-half clockwise with the attached yarn.

STEP 2: Put the loop on the end of the left-hand needle.

STEP 3: Pull the yarn so that the new stitch is snug against the knitting, but not so tight on the needle that you are unable to knit the stitch. Continue to add stitches required by the pattern.

1.

2.

3.

Combine Stitches

Combining Stitches is a way of working stitches from two needles onto one. When used while knitting a simple ribbed fabric, it creates the pleats seen in Drifting Pleats. When using Combine Stitches while knitting around, it allows you to create more unusual shapes, such as flanges, corners, twists and waves from what would otherwise be a simple tube shape.

COMBINE STITCHES IN A K1, P1 RIB
STEP 1: Hold both needles in your left hand.

STEP 2: K1 from the front needle.

STEP 3: P1 from the back needle.

Alternate Steps 2 and 3 until you have combined all of the stitches (or number specified in pattern).

COMBINE STITCHES IN A K2, P2 RIB
Needles are held in the same position as the K1, P1 version, except you alternate K2 from the front needle with P2 from the back needle. The Hourglass scarf uses Combine Stitches in a K2, P2 RIB.

COMBINE STOCKINETTE STITCH
You can also combine two needles onto one needle in a Stockinette stitch pattern. Hold both needles in your left hand with the knit sides facing you. K1 from the front needle, then K1 from the back needle. Repeat until you have combined the desired number of stitches.

1.

2.

3.

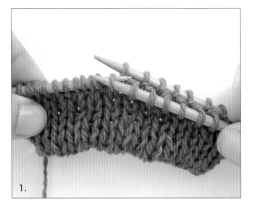

Rib Division

Rib Division is a way of separating the knits and purls of a ribbed fabric onto two different needles and working them separately. Once separated, the stitches can then be worked around to create a tube shape, which when used with Combine Stitches facilitates the creation of flanges, corners, twists and waves found in some of the scarves.

Divide a K1, P1 Rib
Hold knitting in your left hand and 2 empty needles in parallel in your right hand.

Alternate Step 1 and Step 2.

STEP 1: Slip next knit stitch onto the front needle.

STEP 2: Slip next purl st onto the back needle.

Divide a K2, P2 Rib
Hold knitting and empty needles the same way as for dividing the K1, P1 rib. Slip 2 knit stitches to the front needle, followed by 2 purl stitches to the back needle.

Interlocking Stitches

When interlocking stitches, the stitches of a working piece are passed through a finished piece, locking the two pieces together.

In your left hand, hold the finished piece and the working piece together. The working piece is held in front.

STEP 1: Insert the tip of the front (working) needle between the first and second stitch of the finished piece.

STEP 2: Insert the tip of an empty needle, from back to front, through the finished piece in the same location as the front working needle.

Transfer the stitch from the working needle to the back needle.

STEP 3: The stitch has been transferred, and the tip of the needle from Step 1 is returned to the front side.

Transfer the remaining stitches from the front needle to the back needle, progressing across the finished piece. Be sure that all transferred stitches are in the same groove between two garter ridges.

STEP 4: When all stitches are transferred, locking the two pieces together, continue knitting the transferred stitches. You will find the transferred stitches are on the needle backwards when you knit the first row. You can knit them through the front or the back of the stitch to return them to their proper position on the needle.

Intarsia Knitting

The Intarsia technique is used to work blocks of color with separate balls of yarn. When changing from one color to another, you must always bring the new color under and then over the color you have just finished using. In pattern instructions in this book, this is referred to as "twist" or "twist yarns." This twist locks the yarns together and prevents holes. Do not twist the yarns too loosely or there will be either a gap or loose stitches.

Except for Peek, the scarves in this book that require the Intarsia technique are knit in Garter stitch.

KNITTING INTARSIA IN GARTER STITCH

Garter stitch is usually considered a reversible pattern, but when working Intarsia in Garter stitch, there will be a wrong and right side. Always twist yarns on WS when working Intarsia in Garter stitch.

PHOTO 1: When knitting a RS row, both yarns will be in back. Cross the new yarn under and...

PHOTO 2: ...over the yarn you have just finished knitting with.

PHOTO 3: When knitting a WS row, the yarn you have just finished knitting with will be in back. Bring it to the front (WS) between needles. Cross the new yarn under and over the previous color, then between the needles to the back (RS) and continue knitting.

PHOTO 4: RS — shows the clean Intarsia line between colors.

PHOTO 5: WS — shows the twisting from the color change.

Knitting Intarsia in Stockinette Stitch

The purl side is the WS, and yarns should always be twisted on the purl side. When working a purl row, the yarns will be twisted in front. When working a knit row, the yarns will always be twisted in back.

Knitting Intarsia in Reverse Stockinette Stitch

With Reverse Stockinette stitch, the knit side is the WS, so yarns should always be twisted on the knit side. Whether you are on a WS or RS row, first take the yarn to the knit side between the needles.

Working Slip Stitches

Slipped stitches are moved from the left-hand needle to the right-hand needle without knitting them. The stitches can be slipped knitwise or purlwise. Slipping a stitch knitwise will twist the stitch; slipping it purlwise will not. If a pattern does not indicate which way is appropriate, then slip the stitches purlwise.

MULTICOLOR SLIP STITCH PATTERNS

Multicolor slip stitch patterns can range from simple to complex, and are created by the interplay of two colors in a row. Using slip stitches to create these patterns allows you to knit across a row (or around) with a single color, and not carry and work a second color at the same time. Since only one color will be used at a time when knitting a row, there will always be a "working color" yarn and a "non-working color" yarn. The stitches of the non-working color are slipped purlwise, and the working color is carried across the WS of your knitting. Do not pull the working yarn tightly across the slipped stitches or your knitting will pucker. Keep slipped stitches spread comfortably as a guide for the working yarn.

READING SLIP STITCH CHARTS

- The numbers alongside a chart indicate the rows.

- The single square to the right of a row number indicates the "working color" to use for that row.

- The multiple squares on the left are the pattern chart, and indicate which stitches should be knit and which should be slipped. Each square of the pattern chart represents a single stitch. Knit the stitches of the "working color" and slip purlwise all other stitches.

Chart 1, with a single column of row numbers, represents 1-row patterning, in which color changes may be made after every row. These patterns must be worked either by knitting around, or with DPNs in which you must slide your knitting to the opposite end of the needle after each row. All rows will be RS rows.

- The bracketed number below the pattern chart indicates the number of stitches in the pattern. A pattern may require you to repeat a chart across your knitting. This chart could have been written with as few as 2 stitches (squares). If a simple 2-stitch chart were to be worked across 12 stitches, you would be instructed to repeat the chart 6 times.

- A written interpretation of Chart 1 is:
ROW 1 (RS): With Gray yarn, [K1, Slip 1] across 6 sts.
ROW 2 (RS): With White yarn, [Slip 1, K1] across 6 sts.

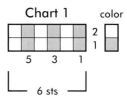

Note: There are many other variations of slip-stitch knitting. If this subject interests you, I suggest you research it further in other books.

Knitting I-Cord

I-Cord is a knitted tube created using two double-pointed needles. Using short Double-Pointed Needles (DPNs), cast on a small number of stitches, about 3 to 6.

Knit all the stitches. Switch needles in your hands, so the needle with the stitches is in your left hand again, with RS facing you. Slide the stitches to the other end of the needle. Pull the yarn across the back of the stitches and knit the next row. Continue this way, sliding and knitting, until the I-Cord is the length you wish.

PHOTO 1: When *not* knitting I-Cord, yarn hangs from the first stitch to be knit.

PHOTO 2: When knitting I-Cord, yarn is attached to stitch farthest from first stitch to be knit.

PHOTO 3: Back of I-Cord with carries visible.

Give the I-Cord a pull and carries across the back disappear. The I-Cord also narrows and lengthens when it is pulled.

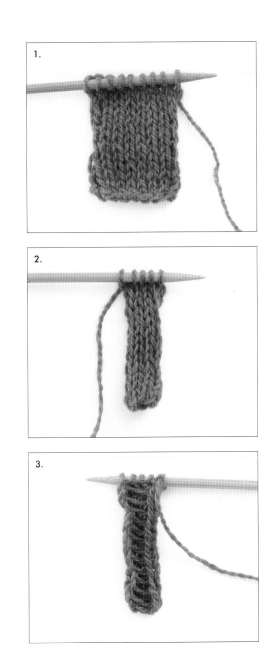

Knitting Around

Knitting around is also referred to as Circular Knitting or Knitting-in-the-Round. Double-pointed needles (DPNs) or circular needles may be used, and the project and/or number of stitches will determine which type of needle is appropriate.

It is critical when knitting around on DPNs or circular needles to keep the cast-on stitches from twisting when you connect them on the first round. If the pattern allows and you choose to, it may be easier to knit one or two rows before you connect and knit around.

A round is equivalent to a row in flat knitting. Exceptions to this are rounds in Linked Rib and Tricorner. In these patterns, when you are knitting flanges or corners, you are actually knitting two rows for each round.

In order to identify the beginning of a new round, place a marker on the needle before the last stitch in a round. Each time you reach the marker as you work around, slip the marker from the left needle to the right needle.

You will notice that a step is formed where you connect ends on the first round and on the bind-off round at the end of your knitting. You can eliminate these steps when you weave in the tails from the beginning and ending of your knitting. Thread a tapestry needle with a tail and insert the tapestry needle into the stitch on the opposite side of the step. Insert the tapestry needle back into the original stitch and pull the tail snug until both sides reach the same level. Weave in the remaining tail and clip.

Knitting Around On Three or More Double-Pointed Needles (DPNs)

Generally, it is easiest to work with your stitches divided onto three needles and knit the stitches with a fourth needle. The three-needle arrangement tends to be more stable, and is not inclined to twist and be unruly, as with four or more needles.

When changing from one needle to the next, it is easier to avoid loose stitches if you insert the empty needle from the following positions.

PHOTO 1: When the next stitch to be worked is a knit stitch, insert the empty needle from below the working needle.

PHOTO 2: When the next stitch to be worked is a purl stitch, insert the empty needle from above the working needle.

As you knit the second stitch after moving from one needle to the next, give the working yarn a firm tug. This will also help eliminate loose stitches where you move from one needle to the next.

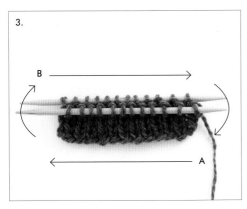

Knitting Around On Two Double-Pointed Needles (DPNs)

This method of Knitting Around is generally used after stitches are divided onto two needles from Rib Division.

The same information about changing from one needle to the next on three or more needles applies to two needles.

PHOTO 3: Knit all stitches on the front needle (A), then turn work so the other side is facing you. Knit the stitches on the second needle (B). Continue knitting around in this manner.

If you are going to work around for more than five rounds, or do not plan on combining stitches onto one needle again, I suggest dividing the stitches over more than two needles.

Scrap Yarn Slits

Scrap Yarn Slits is a technique used to temporarily secure stitches in a piece of knitted fabric so they can be easily accessed later. I used this technique for decorative purposes in this book but it is also functional. For example, it can also be used to make pockets and thumb openings in gloves.

In the patterns, directions will instruct you to "Work SYS across (pattern specified number) sts." In the instructional photos that follow, the knitting is working SYS across 6 sts.

SET UP SCRAP YARN SLITS

STEP 1: Knit stitches with contrasting-colored scrap yarn, preferably of a lighter weight than the project yarn.

STEP 2: Slip the contrasting colored stitches back onto the left-hand needle...

STEP 3: ...and knit them again with the attached yarn. Cut the scrap yarn, leaving a 2" tail.

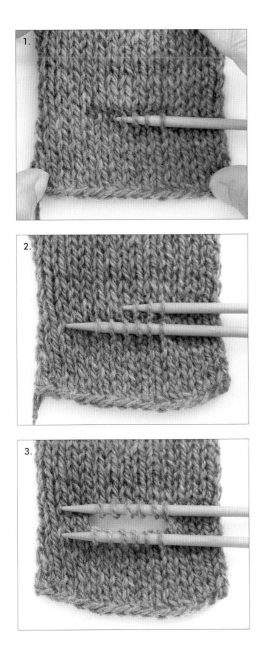

OPEN SCRAP YARN SLITS

When picking up stitches on both sides of
your scrap yarn, use DPNs smaller than the
needles used for your project.

STEP 1: Insert the smaller DPN into each of
the stitches below the contrasting yarn.

STEP 2: Insert another smaller DPN into each
of the stitches above the contrasting yarn.

STEP 3: With the tip of a needle, remove the
contrasting colored stitches. You may cut the
scrap yarn as you remove it, making it easier
to pull it out.

Short Row Shaping

Short Rows make it possible to knit partial rows without leaving holes in your knitting.

WORKING SHORT ROWS IN STOCKINETTE STITCH
The following directions show short rows being worked on a knit row. Work them the same on purl rows, except substitute "knit side" for "purl side" in Step 4.

In pattern directions, these four steps are referred to as W&T, an abbreviation of Wrap and Turn.

First, knit to the place where you will begin your short row. This place will be specified in your pattern, where you will most likely be instructed to knit a certain number of stitches, then W&T.

STEP 1: With the yarn in back, slip the next stitch purlwise.

STEP 2: Bring the yarn between the needles to the front.

STEP 3: Slip the same stitch back to the left-hand needle.

STEP 4: Turn the work and bring the yarn to the purl side between the needles.

HIDING WRAPS FROM STOCKINETTE STITCH SHORT ROWS
On the first row after working a short row, you will need to hide the wrap from the short row shaping.

On a Knit Row:
To hide a wrap, insert the right-hand needle under the wrap. Knit the wrap and wrapped stitch together (see Photos 5 and 6).

On a Purl Row:
Pick up the wrap and place it on the left-hand needle. Purl the wrap and the next stitch together.

WORKING SHORT ROWS IN GARTER STITCH
Work the same as for Steps 1-3 of Working Short Rows in Stockinette Stitch above. When you turn your work, do not bring the yarn back through the needles in Step 4. Leave the yarn to the back to begin knitting.

HIDING WRAPS FROM GARTER STITCH SHORT ROWS
Hide them the same as for Knit Row Wraps, Photos 5 and 6. Occasionally when you work short rows in Garter stitch, it is best not to hide the wraps. It depends on the yarn that is being used. You may notice in some patterns in this book that you are instructed to hide wraps and some you are not. If you substitute yarns, you will have to decide which is appropriate.

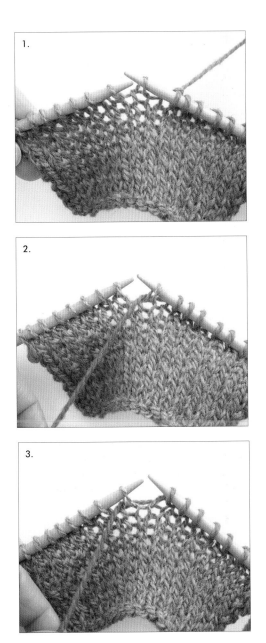

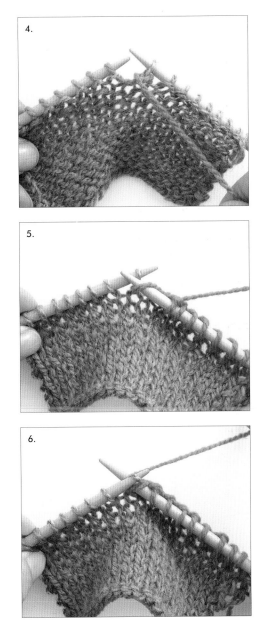

BO	Bind Off
CO	Cast On
DPN(s)	Double-Pointed Needle(s)
K	Knit
K1-f/b	Increase 1 st: Knit into the front, then back of a st.
K1-tbl	Knit 1 through back of loop (st).
K2tog	Knit 2 sts together: Insert right-hand needle knitwise into second and first sts on left-hand needle. Knit the two sts together. This decrease slants to the right.
LLI	Left Lifted Increase: Pick up stitch below last stitch on the right-hand needle and place on left-hand needle. Knit the picked-up stitch.
MC	Main Color (yarn)
Next Needle	The needle following the working needle.
P	Purl
P1-b/f	Increase 1 st: Purl into the back, then front of a st.
P2tog	Purl 2 sts together: Insert right-hand needle purlwise into the first and second sts on left-hand needle. Purl the two sts together.
Previous Needle	The needle preceding the working needle.

RLI	Right Lifted Increase: Pick up stitch below next stitch on the left-hand needle and place on left-hand needle. Knit the picked-up stitch.
RS	Right side (opposite of WS, not left side)
SKP	Slip, Knit, Pass Over: Slip 1 st knitwise from left-hand needle to right-hand needle; knit the next st on the left-hand needle; pass the slipped st over the knit st and off the needle. This decrease slants to the left.
SPN(s)	Single-Pointed Needle(s)
SSK	Slip, Slip, Knit: Slip 2 sts knitwise from left-hand needle to right-hand needle, one at a time; insert tip of left-hand needle in front of both slipped sts and knit them together. This decrease slants to the left.
St(s)	Stitch(es)
St st	Stockinette stitch: knit on the RS and purl on the WS.
SYS	Scrap Yarn Slit (see page 138)
W&T	Wrap and Turn (see Instructions for Short Row Shaping, page 140).
Working Needle	The needle with the attached yarn (working yarn).
WS	Wrong side

Alchemy Yarns
PO Box 1080
Sebastapol, CA 95473
707-823-3276
www.alchemyyarns.com

Blue Sky Alpacas
1815 Viking Blvd. NE
Cedar, MN 55011-9555
888-460-8862
www.blueskyalpacas.com

Classic Elite
122 Western Avenue
Lowell, MA 01851
800-343-0308
www.classiceliteyarns.com

Green Mountain Spinnery
PO Box 568
Putney, VT 05346
802-387-4528
800-321-9665
www.spinnery.com

Habu Textiles and Yarns
135 West 29th Street
Suite 804
New York, NY 10001
212-239-3546
www.habutextiles.com

Harrisville Designs
PO Box 806
Center Village
Harrisville, NH 03450
603-827-3333
www.harrisville.com

Karabella Yarns
1201 Broadway
New York, NY 10001
212-684-2665
800-550-0898
www.karabellayarns.com

Knitting Fever
315 Bayview Avenue
PO Box 336
Amityville, NY 11701
516-546-3600
www.knittingfever.com

Koigu
PO Box 158
Chatsworth, Ontario
N0H 1G0, Canada
519-794-3066
888-765-WOOL
www.koigu.com

Manos Del Uruguay
Design Source
PO Box 770
Medford, MA 02155
888-566-9970
www.manos.com.uy

Peace Fleece
475 Porterfield Road
Porter, ME 04068
207-625-4906
www.peacefleece.com

Rowan Yarns
Westminster Fibers
4 Townsend West, Unit 8
Nashua, NH 03063
603-886-5041
www.knitrowan.com

The Fibre Company
North Dam Mill
2 Main Street
Biddeford, ME 04005
207-282-0734
www.TheFibreCo.com

KNITTING NEEDLES

For some scarves in this book, it's necessary to use US #10¾ (7mm) and 6-inch wooden DPNs. Needles with both these attributes can be found at:

Crystal Palace
www.straw.com/cpy/cpybambo.html

PATTERN WORK

Cheryl Hevey
Pattern proofing and writing
needledexpressions@yahoo.com

Sue McCain
Knitting tech editing and
chart creation
www.vermontfiberdesigns.com

ACKNOWLEDGMENTS

First, I thank Melanie Falick for giving me the opportunity to present my designs to you, and for encouraging me to think beyond aspects of my personal taste. During our first meeting, Melanie's response to my subdued color palette was, "This book is not about what Lynne would wear." That comment became a mantra during the rest of my work on the book. Our first meeting took place in Soho at Joelle Hoverson's store, Purl (www.purlsoho.com), where Joelle generously piled my suitcase full of gorgeous yarns in a red palette (to add punch to my grays). I took it as a challenge to use all the yarns that Joelle provided me with, and succeeded but for two yarns. That meeting helped clarify much for me. Thank you both again.

Next, my thanks goes to two friends, Cheryl Hevey and Bonnie Des Roches, who patiently and thoughtfully critiqued and tweaked (TwK) my first pattern drafts. Trust me, the thought in thoughtfully was great. As for the TwK, I had to put it somewhere in this book. Bonnie and Cheryl insisted I remove it from a pattern and stick with the current conventions for knitting abbreviations. I love to break rules, but this time I complied, knowing they were right.

I also want to thank Sue McCain, the knitting technical editor, who patiently and calmly allowed me to rebel and then afterward helped pull everything together into clear, concise instructions presented in a more time-honored format.

Finally, but not minimally, thanks to my husband, Doug. He rigged up an ingenious little photo studio, so I could take the instructional photos as I worked, clicking away with my foot, while my hands were busy knitting. And he has helped in countless other ways, for which I will be ever grateful.